PAGNOL'S PROVENCE

PAVILION

PAGNOL'S PROVENCE

JULIAN MORE

Photographs
by Carey More

For my grandchildren
Sasha, Manon and Cameron

First published in Great Britain in 1996 by
PAVILION BOOKS LIMITED
26 Upper Ground, London SE1 9PD

Text copyright © Julian More 1996
Photographs copyright © Carey More 1996, except for those
listed below

PICTURE CREDITS
Compagnie Mediterranéenne de Films: p. 79
Gaumont: 54, 58, 66
Photo Henri Moiroud/Private collection MPC: p. 6
Photo Roger Corbeau: pp. 111, 114, 129
Photo Roger Forster from CMF collection: pp. 83, 87
Renn Productions/Ronald Grant Archive: pp. 148, 149, 161

Map drawn by Martin Collins

The author and publishers are grateful to Editions B. de Fallois/
Jacqueline Pagnol for kind permission to reproduce all the
extracts from Pagnol's works quoted in the text. All translations
of Pagnol texts are by the author.

Designed by Carol McCleeve

A CIP catalogue record for this book is available from the
British Library.

ISBN 1 85793 356 7

Typeset in 11/13½ pt Garamond light

Printed and bound in Singapore by Kyodo Printing Co.

2 4 6 8 10 9 7 5 3 1

This book may be ordered by post direct from the publisher.
Please contact the Marketing Department.
But try your bookshop first.

Title page: A lavender field near Valréas,
home town of Marcel Pagnol's paternal
ancestors.

CONTENTS

INTRODUCTION

Near where I live in northern Provence, Pagnols have been around since the French Renaissance.

At the market town of Valréas, Marcel Pagnol's ancestors were craftsmen belonging to various guilds, and a recent member of the family, the late Jean Pagnol, was the town's archivist and wrote *belles lettres*. And at nearby Vaison-la-Romaine, where Marcel's midwife great-aunt delivered his father, Joseph, there is a restaurant called La Bartavelle after that rare and succulent Provençal partridge made famous in *La Gloire de Mon Père*.

The inspiration for Marcel Pagnol's Provençal plays, films, memoirs and novels is further south and east: the Old Port of Marseilles; craggy, herb-scented hills a tram ride from the city centre; the wild uplands of the Alpes de Haute-Provence; and a short stretch of Mediterranean coast. His name is familiar throughout Provence and children are called Manon and Aurélie, Marius and César after his characters. Here and further afield, more than two hundred French schools are named after him. And many new fans have come to know him, in France and all over the world, since the success of the films *Jean de Florette* and *Manon des Sources*.

After the bucolic sentimentalizing and travel poster images of Provence as a region of eternal sun and happy, smiling peasants bearing gifts of peaches and aubergines to second-home owners, Pagnol's bitter-sweet, Greek tragedy of revenge relieved us sharply of our rose-tinted spectacles. He showed us the realities of this paradoxical part of the world with its light and shade, bone-searing winds and blistering heat, sweet perfumes and earthier smells, warm laughter and treacherous moods.

'To reach the universal, stay at home', said Pagnol. Yet, as contradictory as Provence itself, Pagnol himself did not stay at home. Part sophisticated Parisian, part child of the *garrigue*, he was a nomad, seldom spending long periods of time in the region of his birth, preferring to shuttle back and forth on the train, third class, between Paris and Marseilles, in espadrilles and an open-neck shirt with an apple for his luggage; or later in a Hispano-Suiza sports car, driven strictly by himself – he hated being a passenger. He also had a fear of flying and boat trips, and only went abroad twice – to England and Portugal. Travel in France was a mere necessity of a gypsy's life, and temporary homes – whether an apartment in his Marseilles film studios or

Opposite: A cinema in the former chapel of a seventeenth-century convent, Les Visitandines, Forcalquier.

a mansion in Monte Carlo – were his perfect caravans.

His roots went deep, however. Marcel Pagnol, in his evocation of spirit of place, was to Provence what Thomas Hardy was to Wessex. From an intimate knowledge of the Étoile hills and France's second city at the height of its prosperity, he spoke eternal truths with a Marseilles accent. His revolutionary play *Marius* brought Provençals to the Paris stage for the first time, not as lovable provincial buffoons but flesh-and-blood characters with whom even the most critical Parisian, looking snootily down the whole length of the Rhône valley, could identify. It was a triumph, with Pagnol firmly established as a pace-maker.

A misconception exists about his status as a writer. Because of the recent success of his novels and memoirs as films and in translation, it is often assumed by those who know him outside France that Pagnol was a literary lion. Accomplished though he was as prose writer, essayist, and translator (*Hamlet* and *The Bucolics*), he is mainly remembered for his work in the theatre and cinema: eleven plays produced; writer, director, producer – often all three – of eighteen films. Literary acclaim late in life came well after his election to L'Académie Française which, in fact, celebrated his pioneering contribution to French cinema in its Golden Age.

Italian cinéaste, Roberto Rossellini, often considered to have invented neo-realism, later told Pagnol: 'The father of neo-realism in the cinema isn't me, it's you. If I hadn't seen *The Well-Digger's Daughter*, I would never have made *Rome Open City.'* And Orson Welles, soon after his success with *Citizen Kane*, called Pagnol's *La Femme du Boulanger* 'the most beautiful film I have ever seen'.

Much of Pagnol's work has nothing to do with Provence. But his infallible eye for the essence of a given setting and sharp, witty ear for dialogue were most at home there. His Provençal films – as much as the now better-known novels and memoirs – bring spirit of place from a pastis bottle like a genie from a lamp. Pagnol conjures up the Old Port of Marseilles with its camaraderie, ironic laughter, spicy smells, and card games beneath café awnings in the cool of evening. We follow his youthful ramblings in the Étoile hills, share his excitement at each new discovery of bounty and drought. He brings us the wild beauty of perched villages and isolated, upland farms loud with cicadas' summer song and the howl of a winter mistral. And despite his own mistrust of the sea, Pagnol evokes the green-water creeks and cliffs with Aleppo pines jutting sheer out of the rockface and the little fishing ports of his Mediterranean coast like a sailor born.

Our book is not so much a biography as a traveller's companion. Each chapter ends with a practical guide to Pagnol's Provence – what to see and where to stay and eat.

On a voyage of discovery Carey and I visit the places that inspired Pagnol, with their very special smells and tastes and sounds; we see how they have changed, what regional spirit is still there, where the country has remained unspoilt and towns have preserved their identity; above all, we try to convey a picture of Provence that is inimitably Pagnolian.

JULIAN MORE
Visan, 1996

ACKNOWLEDGEMENTS

First, my warm thanks to Jacqueline Pagnol for welcoming me at her Paris home and talking most entertainingly about her late husband's life and work; she confirmed the description of Marcel Pagnol as 'an anxious optimist', a trait he shared with many authors, including this one. My own anxiety soon gave way to optimism in the presence of Madame Pagnol's easy laughter and affectionate reminiscences; and owing also to the help of Pagnol's niece, Marianne Pagnol-Larroux, in authorizing the extensive quotations and putting me right on a number of points.

It was, as always, a pleasure to be accompanied on the Pagnol trail by my daughter, Carey More, who took the photographs.

At Aubagne, we were welcomed and generously advised by Pagnol biographer Georges Berni, who was also our guide on a number of walks. The local fire brigade provided four-wheel-drive transport in the Pagnol hills, and the Aubagne Tourist Board was also most helpful.

The Marcel Pagnol Lycée at St-Loup opened its doors to us to photograph its movie poster collection, thanks to its Professor of English, Maguy Nakache.

Much gratitude also to my wife, Sheila, for suggestions at every stage; to Anne Macrae, for keeping me up to date with local Pagnol events; to my agents, Abner Stein and Sandy Violette, for their usual terrific back-up; to publisher Colin Webb, for his great help in shaping the book; to editor Mandy Greenfield, who saw it patiently through the works; and to Carol McCleeve, who designed it.

Finally, I am most grateful to all the sources that gave me leads.

PAGNOL IN PROVENCE

1895   Marcel Pagnol born at Aubagne near Marseilles, 28 February. Father: Joseph, schoolmaster; mother: Augustine, former dressmaker.

1897   Moves to Marseilles. Joseph appointed to St-Loup school in suburbs.

1898   Birth of brother Paul.

1900   Joseph promoted to Chemin de Chartreux school nearer city centre.

1902   Birth of sister Germaine.

1904   First holidays in the hills near La Treille.

1905   Joseph promoted to Lycée Thiers, Marseilles.

1909   Birth of brother René.

1910   Death of mother. First poems published in literary revue, *Massilia*.

1913   Passes Baccalauréat at Lycée Thiers.

1914   Founds literary revue, *Fortunio*, with schoolfriends. Military service at Nice.

1915   Demobilized as medically unfit. Appointed schoolmaster at Digne, then Tarascon.

1916   Marries Simonne Collin.

1919   English teacher at Lycée Mignet, Aix-en-Provence.

1922   Promoted to Lycée Condorcet, Paris.

1923   First meeting with actress Orane Demazis who later becomes his lover and leading lady.

1927   Gives up teaching. Full-time playwright.

1928   First Paris theatre hit with *Topaze*.

1929   Repeats success with his first Provençal subject, *Marius*.

1930   Birth of son, Jacques, by showgirl Kitty Murphy.

1931   Writes and produces first film, *Marius*, directed by Alexander Korda, starring Toulon-born Raimu, Orane Demazis, and Pierre Fresnay in the title role. Next play in *The Marseilles Trilogy*, *Fanny*, opens in Paris, with Demazis again in the title role.

1932   Film of *Fanny*, directed by Marc Allégret, marks move from theatre to cinema.
Death of brother Paul.

1933   Debut as film director with *Jofroi*, based on story by Provençal novelist Jean Giono.
Birth of son, Jean-Pierre, by Orane Demazis.

1934   Film *Angèle*, also based on Giono story, marks first hit of Marseilles-born actor, Fernandel. Demazis in title role.

1935   Film *Cigalon*.

Birth of daughter, Francine, by Yvonne Pouperon.

1936   Third episode of *The Marseilles Trilogy*, *César*, written first for the 'screen, with the original leading actors.

1937   *Regain*, based on a novel by Giono, stars Fernandel and Demazis. *Le Schpountz* stars Fernandel.

1938   Opening of Studios Marcel Pagnol at Marseilles.
La Femme du Boulanger, starring Raimu and Ginette Leclerc, shot in studios and at Le Castellet.
Love affair with actress Josette Day.

1940   *La Fille du Puisatier* stars Day, Raimu and Fernandel.

1941   Divorce from Simonne Collin.
Buys Château de la Buzine, near Aubagne, as part of Hollywood-en-Provence project – abandoned during German Occupation. Studios sold. Refuses to make films for Germans. Spends duration of war at La Gaude, near Nice, and in the deep France of La Sarthe.

1944   Break with Josette Day.
Love affair with actress Jacqueline Bouvier, first met in 1938.

1945   *Naïs*, based on Émile Zola short story, stars Bouvier and Fernandel.
Marriage to Jacqueline Bouvier, his companion for life.

1946   Birth of son, Frédéric.
Return to Paris theatre with adaptation of *César*.

1947   Election to *L'Académie Française*.

1951   Pagnols settle in Monte Carlo. Birth of daughter, Estelle.

1952   The first *Manon des Sources* stars Jacqueline Bouvier as Manon.

1954   Adaptation of Alphonse Daudet's *Letters from My Windmill*, Pagnol's last film.
Death of daughter Estelle, aged two.

1956   Pagnols move to Paris.

1957–8 Childhood memoirs *La Gloire de Mon Père* and *Le Château de Ma Mère* become bestsellers, establishing Pagnol's literary reputation.

1959   A third volume, *Le Temps des Secrets*, published.

1962   A two-part novel inspired by the film *Manon des Sources* is published as *Les Eaux des Collines: I. Jean de Florette; II. Manon des Sources*.

1974   Death in Paris on 18 April.

1986   Films of *Jean de Florette* and *Manon des Sources*, directed by Claude Berri, star Yves Montand, Gérard Depardieu, Emmanuelle Béart, and Daniel Auteuil.

1990   Film director Yves Robert makes *La Gloire de Mon Père* and *Le Château de Ma Mère*.

1995   The Marcel Pagnol Centenary.

PROVENCE IN PAGNOL

Marcel Pagnol (1895–1974), film-maker, scenarist, playwright, novelist, translator and man of letters, whose motto was 'To reach the universal, stay at home'. Home, for much of his life, was Provence.

THE MARSEILLES TRILOGY

I. Marius (play and film)

César runs the quayside Bar de la Marine in the Old Port of Marseilles. His waiter son, Marius, and the fishwife Honorine's daughter, Fanny, are childhood sweethearts. Marius is jealous of a wealthy widowed sailmaker, Panisse, who wants to marry Fanny. It spurs his ambitions to see the world and, after their nights of love, Fanny and Marius part, he for the South Seas, she for marriage to Panisse.

II. Fanny (play and film)

Panisse welcomes Fanny's child by Marius – as long as it is brought up as his. They marry. Marius returns some months later, and tries to claim the child, Césariot. César persuades his son not to break up a reasonably happy home, and once again Marius leaves Marseilles.

III. César (film and play)

Panisse dies. The now grown-up Césariot learns that he is not Panisse's son but Marius's. He goes in search of the banished

Marius, and – with the help of his grandfather, César – is instrumental in bringing his real parents, Fanny and Marius, together again.

Jofroi (film based on Jean Giono story)

At his farm near Manosque, old Jofroi has sold an orchard to Fonse. When Fonse tries to chop down his beloved trees, Jofroi threatens to commit suicide in order to save them. His suicide attempts put him in danger of mortal sin, but he is saved from this by a natural death. Fonse will keep a few trees in his memory.

Angèle (film based on Giono novel)

Innocent farmer's daughter, Angèle, elopes with Le Louis, a louche itinerant farm worker. She becomes a Marseilles prostitute, has a baby by a sailor, and is rescued by Saturnin, her father Clarius's farmhand. To avoid family disgrace, Clarius imprisons Angèle and her baby in the farm cellar. Once again she is saved – by the love of Albin, an itinerant farm worker who can ignore her past.

Cigalon (short film)

Cigalon, temperamental chef at a village restaurant, refuses to serve Sunday customers. He is only interested in feeding himself, until the arrival of a customer worthy of his culinary arts. But the Count turns out to be a petty crook from Marseilles who can't pay his bill.

Regain (film based on Giono novel)

Visiting the perched village of Aubignane, itinerant knife-grinder Gédémus and his girl Arsule find it deserted and in a state of collapse. Its only inhabitant is Panturle, a gentle giant who survives by poaching. Arsule leaves the mean-spirited Gédémus for Panturle. Together they revive the dying village and others begin to return there.

Le Schpountz (film)

The son of a village storekeeper wants to be a film star. Members of a film company on location in Provence play a cruel trick on him, pretending that a contract awaits him in Paris. Inadvertently, he becomes a success and returns to his village a hero.

La Femme du Boulanger
(film based on Giono story)

The new village baker Aimable has a beautiful young wife Aurélie. Although apparently devoted to her older husband, Aurélie cannot resist the charms of handsome young shepherd Dominique. She runs away with him. Shattered, Aimable can no longer bake. In an act of solidarity, the villagers send out a search party to bring Aurélie back from her brief idyll.

La Fille du Puisatier (film)

Patricia, well-digger Pascal's daughter, becomes pregnant by Jacques, flying-ace son of a wealthy shopkeeper in Salon-de-Provence. Class differences prevail: when Jacques is called up during the Second World War, Pascal cannot persuade Jacques's parents to take responsibility for the child. His family is disgraced. Only when Jacques is 'missing presumed dead' do his parents help bring up the child. Jacques miraculously returns. He and Patricia are reunited, and the child's grandparents take their proper place.

Naïs (film based on short Émile Zola novel)

Hunchback Toine works with Naïs at a brick factory in L'Estaque. In the summer holidays they work together at the Cassis holiday home of a wealthy Aix-en-Provence lawyer, where Naïs's brutally jealous father Micoulin is caretaker. Micoulin finds out about Naïs's affair with the lawyer's son, Frédéric, and tries to kill him. Toine, protective of Naïs, arranges for Micoulin to meet with a fatal accident, and the lovers are saved.

Les Lettres de Mon Moulin (film)

Four of Alphonse Daudet's famous Provençal short stories *Letters from My Windmill* are included in Pagnol's film: 'La Curé de Cucugnan', 'Les Trois Messes Basses', 'L'Elixir du Révérend Père Gaucher', 'Le Secret de Maître Cornille'.

SOUVENIRS D'ENFANCE
(*Memoirs*)

I. La Gloire de Mon Père

Mainly evoking 'the most beautiful days of my life', Pagnol describes his idyllic childhood holidays in L'Étoile hills. He is specially proud when his non-sportive father bags a brace of *bartavelle* partridges.

II. Le Château de Ma Mère

Holiday memories continue: meeting Lili des Bellons, the local boy from whom Pagnol learns about springs, hunting, and the nature of the hills; sheltering from a violent storm in the Big Owl's cave; being threatened by the mean caretaker of the Château de la Buzine and his mother fainting with fear as a result.

III. Le Temps des Secrets

First love and Marseilles schooldays. After infatuation with Isabelle, his 'little Red Queen', Pagnol returns from holidays in the hills to the harsh realities of the Lycée Thiers where he proves to be a natural leader.

IV. Le Temps des Amours

Confessions of a young writer's love life.

L'EAU DES COLLINS
(Two-Part Novel)

I. Jean de Florette

Le Papet, head of the Soubeyran clan, the wealthiest peasants in the village of Les Bastides Blanches, has no son. He grooms his uncouth nephew, Ugolin, to inherit. United in their greed, Le Papet and Ugolin want another property, Les Romarins, for its secret spring. They block it, and cruelly watch the destruction of the new owner, Jean de Florette, whose plans fail for lack of water, leading to his death while blasting a well.

II. Manon des Sources

Manon, Jean de Florette's daughter, avenges her father's death. The Law of Silence prevails in the village; nobody dares accuse the Soubeyrans. So Manon blocks the spring that feeds the village fountain – and also Ugolin's water supply. In the ensuing panic, Manon finds her chance to accuse Le Papet and Ugolin of causing her father's death. Ugolin hangs himself. Le Papet is disgraced. And – the final nail in his coffin – news reaches him that he did in fact have a son of his own: Jean de Florette.

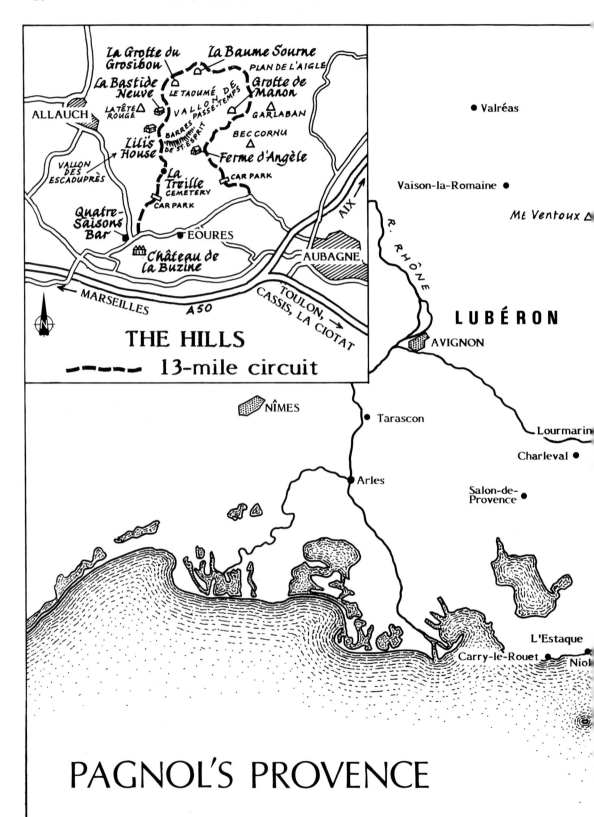

THE HILLS

----- 13-mile circuit

PAGNOL'S PROVENCE

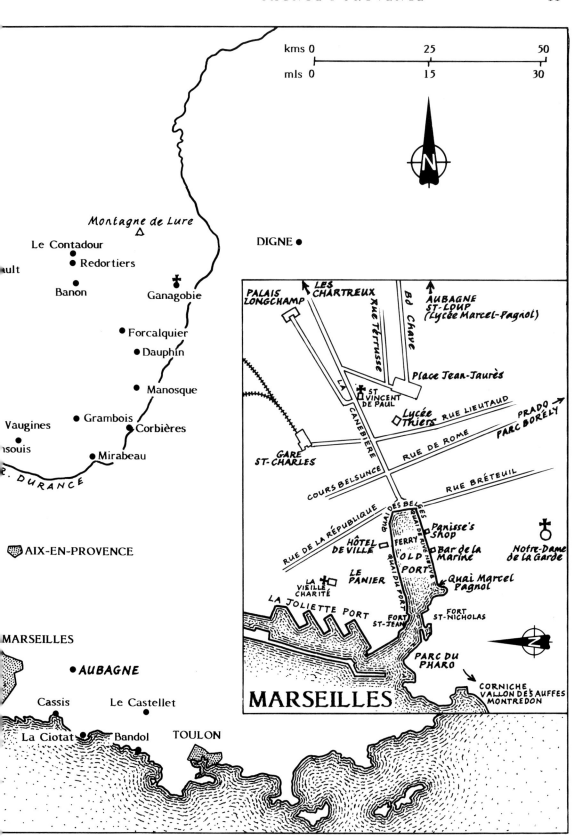

kms 0   25   50

mls 0   15   30

N

Montagne de Lure

Le Contadour

DIGNE

Redortiers

ault

Banon

Ganagobie

Forcalquier

Dauphin

Manosque

Vauginès

Grambois

Corbières

nsouis

Mirabeau

R. DURANCE

AIX-EN-PROVENCE

MARSEILLES

AUBAGNE

Cassis

Le Castellet

La Ciotat

Bandol

TOULON

PALAIS LONGCHAMP

LES CHARTREUX

Rue Térrusse

Bd Chave

AUBAGNE ST-LOUP (Lycée Marcel-Pagnol)

Place Jean-Jaurès

ST VINCENT DE PAUL

LA CANEBIÈRE

Lycée Thiers

RUE LIEUTAUD

PRADO

PARC BORÉLY

GARE ST-CHARLES

RUE DE ROME

COURS BELSUNCE

RUE BRÉTEUIL

RUE DE LA RÉPUBLIQUE

QUAI DES BELGES

QUAI DU RIVE NEUVE

Panisse's Shop

Notre-Dame de la Garde

HÔTEL DE VILLE

FERRY

Bar de la Marine

OLD PORT

LA VIEILLE CHARITÉ

LE PANIER

QUAI DU PORT

Quai Marcel Pagnol

LA JOLIETTE PORT

FORT ST-JEAN

FORT ST-NICHOLAS

PARC DU PHARO

N

CORNICHE VALLON DES AUFFES MONTREDON

MARSEILLES

CHAPTER ONE

AUSPICIOUS BEGINNINGS

Le Bec Cornu, one of Marcel Pagnol's childhood hills in l'Étoile range near Aubagne.

André Pagnol, Marcel's paternal grandfather, hailed from Valréas, a small but important medieval town in northern Provence and a renowned centre of craftsmen's guilds. He was a master stone-cutter. Origins of the family are vague, but from local records it can be assumed they came to Provence from Spain in the sixteenth century. In those days the French registering an immigrant worker called, for instance, 'Juan Hernandez y Casals' simply as 'Jean L'Espagnol' saved a lot of ink and quill scratchings. The patronym 'Espagnol' was eventually shortened to Pagnol.

Just as other foreigners – from yesterday's Greeks and Ligurians to today's British and Americans – find themselves absorbed into the polyglot Provençal culture mix, the Pagnols became sharecroppers on the land of Franciscan friars.

The anti-militarist Marcel recounts gleefully how Pagnol sword-makers, following the military's changing demands in weaponry, became Pagnol gunsmiths – with disastrous results. A great-great uncle, smoking a pipe while filling cartridges, was blown through the closed window of his workshop, 'in a grand finale of sparks, surrounded by whirling suns, borne upon a fountain of roman candles'. The beard on his left cheek never grew again and he was known locally as Lou Rousti, Provençal for 'the Roast'. Henceforth, the family sensibly made cardboard boxes. 'Here was a fine example of Latin wisdom: first they gave up steel, a heavy, hard, and trenchant matter, then gunpowder which is no friend of cigarettes, and consecrated their activity to cardboard, a light and obedient product, soft to the touch and in any event non-explosive' (*La Gloire de Mon Père*).

Grandfather André Pagnol, however, was the odd man out. No one knows why he reverted to heavy matter and became a master stone-cutter. Certainly Marcel inherited his craftsmanship, not only as a writer but as a do-it-yourself fiend, an amateur inventor who could turn his hand to any job around a film set. His canvas director's chair was seldom used – he'd be up some ladder, or helping an electrician fix a lamp, or discussing plans for a custom-built location farmhouse or ruined village with his friend and builder, Marius Brouquier, who was as close to him as his actors.

The grandfather who inspired this practicality was, of necessity, a traveller. Small, broad-shouldered, and with a venerable white beard, André Pagnol did a master craftsman's Tour de France, working in different parts of the country – a professional requirement of *compagnons* of his guild.

Eventually, the boom city of Marseilles, gateway to the Orient and Africa under Napoleon III's gilt-edged imperial rule which saw the opening of the Suez Canal, brought André to work on the ever-expanding docks. He settled there with his wife, Eugénie, and six children.

Family honour, Marseilles style, is a recurrent theme of Pagnol's drama – with a touch of Greek hubris appropriate to that city's Phocian origins. Angelic babies born the wrong side of the blanket proliferate in his plays, films, and novels: among them, the long-suffering Fanny's son, Césariot, whose water-front origins do not prevent him majoring as a brilliant engineer at the exclusive Parisian Polytéchnique; the farmgirl-turned-prostitute Angèle's baby boy is step-fathered by a willing, kindly young peasant from the highlands of Haute-Provence where men treat innocent farmgirls more honourably than do Marseilles *mecs*; and Florette's ill-starred hunchback son, Jean, is avenged by his daughter, Manon, as the force of destiny works its ineluctable Olympian justice.

Whatever tragedies are encountered along the rocky paths of Provence, happy endings are inevitably the lot of Pagnol's mythic love-children. They reflect his own sunny childhood, although his origins as son of a happily married schoolteacher and dressmaker were impeccably legitimate.

His paternal grandfather, however, may have contributed the more adventurous genes. André's one recorded infidelity to Marcel's grandmother is chronicled with sympathetic humour in *Le Temps des Secrets*. All other male relatives seem to have led blamelessly bourgeois sex lives, so Marcel must also have inherited André's appreciation of women. Four serious *amours*, two wives, three children born out of wedlock, and two by his second wife made Marcel particularly compassionate to the peccadillo of grandfather André.

Marcel was a great raconteur. Café-owners loved to install him at a particularly advantageous corner table from which he could regale the customers with witty anecdotes, providing free entertainment in days before the drone of bar TV. One can easily picture him, expatiating with relish on grandfather André's visit to Paris after the 1870 Franco-Prussian War, as he records it in *Le Temps des Secrets*: 'At that time, Paris was a lot further from Marseilles than Moscow is today. . .'

As a member of the *Compagnons des Bouches-du-Rhône*, André was recruited to repair war damage to the Hôtel de Ville. More than a mere mason (craftsmen he denigrated for hiding stone with mortar), he was an artist capable of carving the dovetails and Jove's thunderbolts beloved of nineteenth-century civic art. As for the Paris town hall's ornate bell-turrets, 'nearly all these *chefs d'oeuvre* were wounded or mutilated, and some had collapsed in pieces on the roof'.

At the *Compagnons'* hostel, far from his beloved Eugénie, André entertained the assembled company as his grandson was later to do. 'My grandfather was Provençal. He sang Christmas carols beautifully, and more often serenades. He was an easy laugher, and during the short evenings round the fire, he would tell tales of love.' His charm was irresistible. Like a troubadour, André found his temporary lady love in the comely shape of the hostel's manageress, a woman of 'middling good virtue'. He was lonely, and a brief fling was inevitable. Unfortunately, a jealous colleague, returning to Marseilles for a stint at the docks, shopped André to Eugénie. Although the trusting wife didn't believe a word of it and sent the traitor packing with a knee in the balls, a nagging suspicion that André's persistent denials were white lies made it a much-picked bone of contention. Eventually, Eugénie promised never to speak of it again. 'But she talked of nothing else, even when she thought she wasn't talking about it, and the cross-examination, begun in 1871, continued to 1907.'

Then came the climax, in their retirement farmhouse at Roquevaire near Aubagne. He was eighty-six, she two years younger – with a single, precious remaining tooth. One evening, Eugénie reckoned André was getting a cold and needed a little something to fight it off. As a stone-worker, he had drunk his litre of wine a day but never touched spirits, let alone pastis. But that night, ostensibly to fight off the cold, Eugénie laced his thyme infusion with *marc de Provence*. Then she produced a dusty bottle of champagne from the sideboard, reminding her husband that it was their sixtieth wedding anniversary. André asked if she'd forgive him for not helping her to finish the bottle.

'"Whyever not?" asked Eugénie, a little impatiently. "Are you afraid of becoming an alcoholic? At eighty-six, you won't be one for long!"'

So they finished the bottle together. He sang. They danced a polka.

Then, as soon as he was exhausted and well plied, Eugénie finally asked him once more about the Paris fling. The worst there could be between them was a lie. She went down on her arthritic knees to him, begging and beseeching him to tell the truth.

Finally, he confessed. And the more he confessed, the more she wanted to know. 'So he told her how one night the woman had come into his room, and how she bit him while clawing at his shoulders, and she fell on to the bed laughing, her fine feet in the air. . .'

Marcel recalls how, later that night, his parents were urgently summoned by Aunt Fifi to the farm at Roquevaire. The boy went with them. They arrived at dawn, when a surrealist scene of Midi domestic violence greeted them.

In front of the low house, under the big fig tree, there was a group of peasant men and women.

> Four men were holding my grandmother by the shoulders and wrists, and several women formed a barrage round her, hands held out. Dragging the men, she threw herself forward against the women who pushed her back. . . Her eyes were a mad woman's, and she was as strong as a blacksmith.
>
> In the huge Provençal kitchen, there were a number of people, too. . . In the middle of the circle, my grandfather sat on a chair, naked from the waist up. On his feeble chest, long white hairs. Leaning over him, a doctor in glasses, armed with a watch repairer's tweezers, was searching his bleeding shoulder. He was looking for the tooth, the magnificent tooth of my grandmother. . .

And he found it.

Grandfather André, in a state of terrified shock, warned young Marcel to beware of women. His grandmother had become a homicidal, dangerous lunatic. But his mother, Augustine, knew better. His wife was not mad, Augustine assured the old man.

'We heard a long, animal cry, a cry trembling with rage and despair.

'"Listen," said my grandfather, "you don't call that madness?"

'"No," said my mother. "That's love."'

In spite of his strength and creative flair, André Pagnol could hardly read or write. So he saw to it that his children had the best possible education. All six became teachers.

Marcel couldn't have been luckier with his balanced family background. From his grandfather he inherited the physical strength, sensuality and creative ability; from his father, the intellectual love of books, learning and nature; and from his mother, a warmth of heart, and an instinctive understanding of people.

Joseph Pagnol was 'a dark young man, of slight build without being small. He had a fairly pronounced but perfectly straight nose, which happily was shortened at each end by moustache and glasses whose oval lenses were encircled by thin bands of steel. His voice was serious and pleasant and his bluish black hair curled naturally on rainy days' (*La Gloire de Mon Père*).

Marcel's father was passionately devoted to the French state educational system and the fierce anti-clericalism of teachers' colleges. Not for nothing, he claimed, had two Borgias been popes; Avignon, under the Papacy, had made Sodom and Gomorrah look as chaste as the Courts of Love. Though by no means priggish, he had the kind of laic prejudice which believes that Provençal curés debauched village maidens by seducing them with the demon alcohol. They were no better than the Marquis de Sade, with his under-age Marseilles prostitutes at the Lacoste château.

Royalty was Joseph's third *bête noire*. His Unholy Trinity were the Church, Alcohol, and Royalty.

Augustine Pagnol was a practising Catholic, but her disposition was gentler and her frail health made her preserve her energy. This disguised a certain independence of spirit. Joseph never even knew that she had secretly had Marcel baptized.

Like André Pagnol, her father had been a *compagnon* – a steamboat mechanic from Coutances in Normandy who had settled in Marseilles during his Tour de France. He died of yellow fever, while fixing a broken-down ship in Rio de Janeiro. He was only twenty-four. His widow's three children were forced to fend for themselves early in life; Augustine was a dressmaker before her marriage to Joseph.

After completing the young teacher's usual punishing trek of schools in Marseilles slums and villages in the depth of Provence, Joseph was rewarded with promotion to Aubagne, then a small country town eleven miles east of Marseilles. In the first words of *La Gloire de Mon Père*:

> I was born in the town of Aubagne, beneath the Garlaban with its crown of goats, at the time of the last goatherds.
>
> Garlaban is an enormous tower of blue rocks, stuck on the edge of the Plan de l'Aigle, the immense rocky plateau which dominates the green valley of the Huveaune.
>
> The tower is a little wider than it is high, but as it rises from the rock at six hundred metres altitude, it climbs high into the sky of Provence, and sometimes,

in the month of July, a white cloud rests on it for a moment.

The Pagnol apartment was in a tall, noble house on the best street in town, 16 Cours Barthélemy. It is a wide avenue shaded by plane trees, named for the Abbé Barthélemy, a local author of some distinction, who was elected to the twenty-fifth chair of the French Academy in 1789. Always a good liar, Marcel Pagnol claimed that it was to the very same chair in this pantheon of literary and intellectual 'Immortals' that he himself was elected in 1947, the first ever member whose work was mainly associated with the cinema. It showed France's proper and eternal respect for the Seventh Art.

In those days, the Cours Barthélemy was also the scene of keen *boules* games, where tempers were as quick to ignite and fizzle out as firecrackers. Marcel witnessed the strict verification of the winning *boule* with a piece of string: 'My father, among other giants, made prodigious leaps and threw a lump of iron from unimaginable distances. Sometimes there was loud applause, then the giants always ended in an argument, on account of a piece of string they ripped from each other's hands, but they never came to blows' (*La Gloire de Mon Père*).

Some thirty years later, Pagnol had not forgotten the image and sound, putting it to good use in the film of *Fanny*. Shattered by the unannounced departure of his son, Marius, for the South Seas, César is in no mood for losing at *boules*. He has no hesitation in holding up a tram, clattering its way through a leafy suburb of Marseilles, while he measures the position of his *boule* planted firmly between the rails. Furious with his cronies, who are worried for his sanity, César thwacks an entirely blameless onlooker with an umbrella and jumps on the departing tram to escape a loser's humiliation.

Boules is the cricket or baseball of the Midi. At La Ciotat, the nearby naval dockyard town on the Mediterranean coast, a new form of the game, *pétanque*, was developed in 1910. Its inventor found the three paces' dash before throwing one's *boule* too exhausting on a hot summer's evening, and henceforward took aim from a standing position, knees bent.

More importantly for Marcel Pagnol, La Ciotat was also where Augustine felt her first birth pangs. It had been a difficult pregnancy, and Joseph persuaded Augustine to go and stay with his sister, Marie, at La Ciotat, where she was – naturally for a Pagnol – headmistress of the local school. The sea air in a limpid January light and walks on the beach at sunset when the fishermen hoisted their sails would help calm Augustine down.

Boules *players near the*
Cassis waterfront.

'When I think that you did this to me!' had been her none-too-
gentle reproach.

Joseph used to visit her every Saturday on the baker's bike,
armed with goodies to satisfy her cravings. 'He brought almond
biscuits, frangipane tarts, and a sack of white flour to make
pancakes and *beignets. . .*'

Colour returned to Augustine's cheeks, and she needed all
her restored health for the ride back to Aubagne for the birth.
No autoroute in those days: six miles of bumpy road by horse
and buggy, slipping and sliding on patches of ice, were
gruelling for a woman in labour. Augustine very nearly gave
birth at the halfway village, La Bédoule, but she held off, and
Marcel was born in the family apartment in Aubagne where
Augustine 'had finally planted her nails into Joseph's strong
arm'. A birth much like any other, finally. But there was more to
it than that.

A strange coincidence accompanied the coming of Marcel
Pagnol. Perhaps he himself, with his Greek sense of drama,
would have preferred to think of it not so much as a coincidence as a portent. For Pagnol mythology has it that on the very
same day that his mother's labour started, 28 February 1895, in
the very same town of La Ciotat, the motion picture was born.
The brothers Lumière, pioneers of cinematography, were
causing great excitement among passengers and employees of

the Paris–Lyon–Méditerranée line by filming *The Arrival of the Train at the Station of La Ciotat.*

Who cares if a previous Lumière production, *The Waterer Watered*, had been shown a year previously in Paris? Marcel Pagnol was born – more or less – with the silver screen. The stars were in the ascendant for the Seventh Art, and Marcel would one day be directing many of its children along the very same short stretch of coastline where his mother had spent her pregnancy.

There was the great, irascible, warm-hearted Raimu, who immortalized the Marseilles waterfront as César, emperor of the Old Port, his palace the Bar de la Marine.

His son Marius (also a Pax Romana name; Marius was the general who freed their colony of Provincia – Provence – from the Barbarian hordes) was played by a young and dashing Pierre Fresnay. In the last episode of *The Marseilles Trilogy, César,* the prodigal son returns. And off the port of Toulon, near the lighthouse, Marius goes fishing with his own son, Césariot.

Pagnol's attention to local detail is, as usual, meticulous: they hope to find the rockfish peculiar to that coast, the best for a good, pungent fish soup, requiring special bait: *mouredus* to catch a *rascasse*; *esques* for *girelles, royales, lazagnes* and *sarans.*

'Garlaban is an enormous tower of blue rocks, stuck on the edge of the Plan de l'Aigle, the immense rocky plateau which dominates the green valley of the Huveaune' (La Gloire de Mon Père).

Then there was Fernandel in *Naïs* (1945), a Midi Quasimodo protecting Naïs from her mean father on the cliffs above the little fishing port of Cassis. You can almost smell the pine needles, and cicadas gave unpaid performances for the soundtrack. The water glistens way, way below in the narrow creeks known as *calanques*. The Midi sun works its magic, even in black and white.

Pagnol's wife, Jacqueline Bouvier, plays Naïs with charming insouciance, an idealized peasant girl in gingham and a flowery straw hat perched on a mass of blonde curls. Pagnol's films tended to put women – often mother or daughter figures – on a pedestal in the Mediterranean manner. While thirties Hollywood gave Bette Davis, Greta Garbo and Shirley Temple top billing, Pagnol's heroines invariably took second place to the males, however central to the story they were. But in casting pivotal roles like Fanny with the touchingly natural Orane Demazis, Pagnol used the same yardstick of authenticity as he did with his males – Raimu, Fresnay, Fernandel and others.

The birth pangs at La Ciotat signalled the beginning of a long love affair between a creative titan and the infinitely varied world he grew up in. From the stark, grey rockiness of *garrigue* to Virgilian olive groves and shady pine woods, from the spicy, garlicky tang of waterfronts to warm, cerulean waters, from perched village to vibrant city, Provence was imbued with the spirit of the new-born child and marked out for the future pen and camera of Marcel Pagnol.

PAGNOL'S PROVENCE

Surrounding the 9,069 inhabitants of **Valréas**, home town of Marcel Pagnol's antecedents, is a lush plain of Côtes-du-Rhône vineyards set against a backdrop of the first serious hills between the Rhône valley and the Alps, sometimes sprinkled with snow in winter. In high summer the yellow of sunflowers, the purple of lavender, and the green of vineyards form a tapestry in adjoining fields. For one night in August, the whole town smells as though it has been doused in toilet water. Carnival floats made of lavender parade in the Corso de Lavande, led by nubile, mini-skirted drum majorettes, who are as enticing on a hot night as Manon of the Springs, dancing her naked, pagan dance.

Even though Marcel Pagnol himself wasn't born there, Valréas displays a Pagnolian regard for children. Indeed, it calls itself 'the medieval city whose prince is a child' – a reference to yet another colourful summer celebration, the Night of Le Petit St-Jean. Every year, on 23 June, candles are lit in the windows of tall houses in the Place Pie in front of Notre-Dame de Nazareth church; suddenly, amid much pageantry, trumpets sound through the church doors and a five-year-old boy rides out on a white horse to be crowned 'king' of the town for a year. Symbolizing the Lamb of God and Eternal Youth triumphant, the child king is traditionally chosen from among the poorest children in town.

By the nineteenth century the Pagnols would not have qualified; they were already established as well-to-do artisans. Such notables would inevitably find themselves elected to the honourable *guigne-cèbes*, a select self-appointed body of older Valrésians 'looking at onions', as the Provençal expression goes. It means keeping a discreet watch on your neighbours to see that they conform with the town's traditions.

For stopovers at Valréas choose between the Grand Hotel (moderate) and, more interestingly, La Roseraie (expensive) at nearby Grignan (the château once housed the Marquise de Sévigné). My choice would be to stay with a winemaker friend of mine, René Sinard whose wife runs an excellent Bed & Breakfast (inexpensive; clean, modern rooms in an old house, with superb homemade jams for breakfast); or at Baume de Transit's eighteenth-century farmhouse, Domaine St-Luc, where an excellent dinner is provided, wine included (moderate).

It is worth making the detour through ravishing country for dinner in **Vaison-la-Romaine**, the birthplace of Marcel Pagnol's father. There are a number of choices, including La Bartavelle (moderate), which has several Pagnolian menus and a décor of movie stills. La Gloriette (moderate) at Merindol-les-Oliviers has a Pagnolian bakery.

Like so many southern French towns, **Aubagne** has been the victim of a population explosion – from around 9,000 at the time of Pagnol's birth in 1895 to 40,000 today. It absorbed French settlers from Algeria after the War of Independence, and all shades and nationalities of immigrant worker during the nostalgically remembered boomtime.

Now, although inevitable urbanization has encroached on the natural beauty of the Huveaune valley, Aubagne would take exception to being called a suburb of Marseilles. It may be hard to tell where one ends and the other begins, but Aubagne has a life of its own.

Marseilles loucheness is tempered with country innocence. There's a wild, dark, Romany look to many of the faces in the

The festival of Le Petit St-Jean, every 23 June at Valréas, in which a young boy of the town is crowned 'king' for a year.

'The Little World of Marcel Pagnol' – santons *(terra cotta figurines) of the writer's best-loved characters, from a display at Aubagne Tourist Office.*

Opposite: Plage de l'Arène Clos, Cassis, near the spot where Marcel Pagnol made the film of Émile Zola's novel Naïs.

vital, ethnically mixed community. Disconcertingly, they reflect both a warm welcoming and a deep suspicion of outsiders, whether they be Parisian, Dutch, North African, or from the next village.

On the crowded, sunny Cours Barthélemy where Pagnol's father once played *boules*, there is still a genuine, old-fashioned shellfish stall competing with Le Fast Food restaurants. If you stray into the quiet, narrow streets of the old town, it is pleasantly surprising to find that all is not lost to the bulldozer. The Bibliothèque Marcel Pagnol is a fine modern public library with helpful staff and a copious Pagnol dossier for researchers.

Aubagne's main claim to fame at the time of Pagnol's birth was, like Valréas, its connection with a holy child – in this case, the Infant Jesus. His birth was celebrated by artisans in this 'capital of terra cotta' by the making of *santons*, delicately crafted and painted figurines of the Christmas story. Some sixteen master *santonniers* of Aubagne still produce the 'little saints' (*santons*) who followed the star to the stable. Not only are Jesus, Mary, Joseph and the Wise Men in the crèche, but local figures of Provençal folklore wearing clearly recognizable costumes – the Shepherd, the Farmhand, the Miller, the Tambourine-Player, the Mayor and the Curé, the Knife-Grinder, the Lavender-Seller and the Fishwife. All have their own local names (Barnebéou, Le Ravi, Roustido and Pistachié). Many of Pagnol's characters seem to be earthier, more realistic versions of these traditional figures. Fanny the Fishwife, for example; several curés (notably in *La Femme du Boulanger, Jofroi* and *César*); two mayors (aristo in *La Femme du Boulanger*, café-owner in *Jean de Florette*); and the horse-faced, genial Fernandel played both a knife-grinder (*Regain*) and a farmhand (*Angèle*).

The Aubagne Tourist Board Office has its own Pagnol *santons*. Verdi's haunting overture to *The Force of Destiny*, used to such effect in Claude Berri's films, can be heard in the background. Senior citizens, eager schoolchildren or tourists on the Pagnol trail spot their favourites in 'The Small World of Marcel Pagnol', an impressive *santon* display of scenes and characters from his films and plays. Otherwise known as 'Pagnolia', this is a world set in the hills above Aubagne, to which the Tourist Board organizes thirteen-mile or six-mile treks (see Chapter III, pages 68–71), visiting the sites described factually in *La Gloire de Mon Père* and *Le Château de Ma Mère* and fictitiously in *Jean de Florette* and *Manon des Sources*. In a small-scale setting of vales, dales and villages, even the villains like Le Papet and Ugolin are affectionately displayed as 'little saints'.

Aubagne also pays homage to its cinéaste son by housing the Image and Sound Faculty of the University of Provence, which trains audio visual students who are no doubt deep into Virtual Reality. A Youth Video Festival takes place each autumn. On a lighter level, a high summer Festival of Laughter brings international gagsters to town. And there is, of course, the free show of the Saturday market, Provençal but with a Marseilles accent – several decibels louder, the taste and smells stronger, and the vendors even more outrageous: their aubergines, red mullets or guineafowls are claimed to be the best not only in

Provence but in the whole wide world. Newcomers to the Pagnol trail will have their first experience of Marseilles exaggeration: its people are constantly and extravagantly challenging each other's opinions about everything under the sun, whether it be a football manoeuvre or a recipe for *bouillabaisse*.

Aubagne offers the heaviest concentration of Pagnol sites but the least attractive choice of hotels and restaurants. I recommend staying at Gémenos, a comparatively peaceful town a few minutes away in the lush valley of St-Pons. The Relais de la Magdeleine (expensive) has country house style, a charming host and an excellent restaurant. The Hôtel du Parc (moderate) is very friendly and you can relax in the garden after a hike in the Pagnol hills. Eat inexpensive and gingery Vietnamese food at the Lune de Chine in the main street.

Look one way at **La Ciotat** and you see nothing but the grey gantries of naval dockyards; look the other and there's an inviting panorama of mirror-like, misty sea in the vast sweep of the bay east to Bandol. The peaceful little fishing harbour gives not a hint of the industrial problems surrounding the sad closing of the dockyards. Early morning is best. Fishermen mend their nets, and Pagnolian types read *Le Provençal* and *Le Marseillais* over coffee and croissants at the Bar Cristal on the waterfront.

The beach where Augustine Pagnol went into labour has pioneered 'non-stick sand' – a new kind of artificial sand which does not stick to bodies covered in suntan lotion. Where the pioneering Lumière Brothers filmed the train arriving at the station in 1895, old-fashioned travellers by night train from Paris still emerge from the tunnel to that first breathtaking glimpse of the Mediterranean.

CHAPTER TWO

MARSEILLES YOUTH

*Night on Le Vieux Port, Marseilles, with
the church of Notre-Dame-de-la-Garde
floodlit on its hill.*

*T*he Pagnol family were constantly on the move, and within the confines of the French education system, Joseph moved like a rocket, upwards and onwards: first to the village school of St-Loup, today a suburb of Marseilles. The Pagnol budget was helped by a useful local tradition: when a family killed a pig, they always gave sausages, trotters and chops to the local schoolteacher; and Augustine could grow her own garlic, courgettes, tomatoes and aubergines in their little garden.

It was 1897, the year of Marseilles poet Edmond Rostand's Paris triumph with *Cyrano*, who became one of Marcel's early literary heroes, along with Buffalo Bill and the detective Nick Carter. He was a precocious reader. Not even five, he was left by Augustine in Joseph's class while she went to the market. It was a reading lesson. Marcel watched his father writing on the blackboard: 'The mother punished her little boy who was not good.' And, as those who have seen Yves Robert's film of *La Gloire de Mon Père* will remember, Marcel piped up from the back of the class: 'That's not true!' Imagine the astonishment of Joseph to find his four-year-old had 'caught' reading like other children catch measles.

> When my mother returned, she found me in the middle of four teachers, who had sent their pupils into the playground, and were listening to me slowly deciphering the story of Tom Thumb. But instead of admiring this exploit, she went pale, plonked her packages on the floor, shut the book, and carried me away in her arms, murmuring: 'My God, my God. . .'

To the chagrin of the proud father, Augustine thought that he must be ill.

In 1900 Joseph was once again promoted – to the city's biggest school, the Chemin des Chartreux. Once again, like academic gypsies, the family decamped to a lodging provided by the school behind the building in Rue du Jardin-des-Plantes. On health grounds, Augustine discouraged Marcel from reading his father's books; Racine and Shakespeare might bring something on. But so desperate was he for literature that, one day, Augustine found him in the kitchen, deep in a cookery book.

Joseph celebrated the turn of the century with a rousing, socially conscious speech to his pupils about the wonders in store for them – gaslight, motorized public transport, and the ten-hour working day.

Contrary to the stereotypical image of the Marseillais as sun-soaked, work-shy layabouts, the many had never worked harder for the profit of the few. The *belle époque* saw Marseilles at the height of its prosperity. In the newly rich bourgeois hinterland, away from the raunchy port and ramshackle fishing villages of the Corniche, had grown a city to rival Paris in elegance and fine buildings. Its look mirrored the Second Empire, the most recent period of Marseilles expansion. The lavish showiness of Napoleon III's monuments, palaces, churches, promenades and fountains paid tribute to the profiteers of Empire, the shipping magnates, merchants, and owners of import-export houses. The rich needed soap to keep clean, the poor absinthe to keep going. Marseilles soapmakers and Ricard flourished.

Both industries required water: the establishing shot of Marseilles in the film of *La Gloire de Mon Père* shows the Palais Longchamp, the most ornate monument of the period. In fact, its baroque fountains and crescent-shaped colonnades disguised the terminal of the canal bringing the waters of the river Durance to the city. Practical and decorative, it typified the architectural mores of the time.

The main railway station, too, was a noble edifice. In *Angèle*, we see Fernandel, as the farmhand Saturnin, arriving at the Gare St-Charles with a huge bunch of genista from the hills to begin his search for his master's lost daughter. He is no country bumpkin; dignified and well dressed, he strides confidently down the long flight of steps so well known to departing and arriving Marseillais. In the dappled sunlight of the avenue he asks a shopkeeper for directions. 'Don't tell me which street to take next,' says Saturnin, confused, 'I'll forget which one to take first.'

The warren of narrow streets was complemented by new wide avenues like the Rue Impériale, now Rue de la République; and, of course, the splendid Prado, which led to the villas of the rich, standing in secluded gardens of lemon trees, wisteria, palms, and tinkling fountains. A tram occasionally squeaked and rattled by, like the one taking Marcel and his Tante Rose to a favourite childhood haunt, the Parc Borély.

'It was a place to discover shady walks beneath ancient plane trees, wild thickets, lawns which invited you to roll in the grass, park-keepers to prevent you, and ponds navigated by flotillas of ducks' (*La Gloire de Mon Père*).

While Marcel fed the ducks, his spinster aunt was courted by a rubicund gentleman with a bowler hat and leather gloves – clearly a rich toff from a Prado mansion. Soldiers flirted with nannies; children were reprimanded by park-keepers; and the

Overleaf: The Palais Longchamp, Second Empire opulence in a Marseilles monument that combined Art and Natural History museums with a tower of the city's water supply.

band played on. Oncle Jules made considerable headway with
Tante Rose, partly because of his generosity to Marcel, who was
kept quiet with balloons and buggy rides, and partly because he
was the owner of the park. Both Marcel and his aunt were duly
impressed – especially when Jules went down on one knee and
proposed to her. In Yves Robert's film we see them waltzing
romantically, two lone figures against a bandstand in the rain.

Augustine was worried about her twenty-six-year-old sister
marrying an old crock of thirty-seven. But owners of parks
didn't grow on trees, Marcel thought. Tante Rose should grab
him.

Then came Marcel's first disillusionment with grown-ups:
playing hide-and-seek with his younger brother, Paul, he
overheard a family conversation in which Oncle Jules was
referred to not as the owner of the Parc Borély, but as an official
at the Préfecture. An *official* – not even a police inspector!
Marcel's respect for him had to be regained with many presents.
Oncle Jules, whatever he did in the company of *flics*, was still
rich by Joseph's standards.

The *quartier* where the Pagnols lived may not have been the
Prado but it was pleasant enough, and typical of the villages
within the city, inhabited by the petit bourgeoisie. La Plaine-St-
Michel (now Place Jean-Jaurez) was a big, sunny square with a
morning vegetable market. Road-sweepers, well-oiled at the
corner bar, swept away the wilting debris. And, Marcel
remembers, mothers came out to breast-feed their babies in the
limpid winter sun. The Pagnols never lived in any other district.
If they made a move – and they often did – it was to another,
more spacious apartment near by, to cope with a growing
family (Germaine was born in 1902, René in 1909). Eventually
they settled at 51, Rue Térrusse, a roomy, ground-floor flat, well
lit from the back by a little garden.

Everyone knew everyone else. Round the corner was the
Chave Theatre, where the amateur actors included a M. et Mme
Contandin. Their son, Fernand, later became a professional
singer at the Alcazar Music Hall. His fiancée's mother always
referred to him as her daughter's prize possession – 'Her
Fernand' (*Fernand d'elle*), and the name stuck. Fernandel and
Marcel Pagnol, though they never met in those days, lived a
mere block or so from each other.

Tante Rose and Oncle Jules lived a walking distance away in
Rue des Minimes. Their house was fitted with *le gaz*, which
gave them social cachet; they also had a maid. Every Sunday,
after Mass, they came to lunch, and Oncle Jules brought bottles
of wine from his family's vineyard in the Rrrr-oussillon, as he

used to call it, rolling his r's in the manner of people from that region. For Joseph, it was bad enough that Jules had been to Mass, let alone brought wine. Their common bond of hunting was yet to be discovered, and a subtext of polemic seethed below the polite Sunday conversation. Sometimes it erupted.

> My father and he made a good pair of friends, although Oncle Jules, older and richer, sometimes could be patronizing.
> He protested from time to time about the undue length of school holidays.
> 'Admittedly,' he said, 'children have need of a long rest. But in the meantime, teachers could be put to some other work!'
> 'Oh yes,' my father said ironically, 'for two months they could go and replace bureaucrats at the Préfecture, exhausted by their siestas. . .' (*La Gloire de Mon Père*).

The women kept the peace. Tante Rose was pregnant. Marcel, bored by the slowness of his fellow-readers and by the fact-packed, parrot-spouting lessons of primary school, went into the whole question of how babies were born. He reckoned his mother had unbuttoned her navel for his sister Germaine, and now Tante Rose would likewise 'unbutton'.

The last thing Joseph wanted was '*Crapaud*', as he called Marcel affectionately, to be bored at school. As 'the teacher's son', he had to be a performer. Two routes were open to him: senior primary school where, after three years, there was a competition for entry to the top secondary school of the region, a factory for future teachers; or the lycée, which guided its alumnae through a labyrinth of abstractions to university, philosophy, and a fluency in the lingua franca of intellectuals, Latin.

Joseph, ambitious for Marcel to do better than him, as all Pagnol sons had done with each succeeding generation, settled for the second course. How Joseph had suffered for having no Latin! Marcel would become a professor, at least.

But first he would need a scholarship. The competition for places was stiff. As the one candidate from the Chemin des Chartreux, he was trained as rigorously as a cyclist for the Tour de France – limbering up for maths, sweating out grammatical analysis, pacing himself on spelling; his father gave him a dictation every breakfast. His 'trainers' never blamed Marcel for the fact that he finished second. It was the fault of a particularly

sneaky problem about metal alloys, which should never have
been set for a scholarship exam. Marcel's was an honourable
second, and he took his place as a day boy at the Lycée Thiers
in 1905.

It was run with military precision. A roll of drums, beaten by
a ferocious little man with waxed moustaches, announced the
break between recreation and class.

> Beneath very old plane trees yellowed by autumn,
> there were already thirty pupils.
>   I noticed immediately five or six Chinese (who
> were in reality Annamites), a negro, and a swarthy
> boy with frizzy hair. I was to learn later that he was
> the son of a powerful Caïd of Algeria (*Le Temps des
> Secrets*).

Marcel was immediately popular with his schoolmates, and
he became their chief, their organizer, their best friend. Good
looks gave you a head start in Marseilles.

As César says of his own son, Marius: 'You can search the Old
Port and you'll maybe find bigger and fatter, but better looking,
never. NEVER' (*Marius*).

Marcel had pure Provençal beauty, both manly and feminine,
earthy and poetic, with big, faintly mocking eyes and long black
hair to which he devoted much time, combing it into a quiff that
looked as if it fell that way unaided. Vanity was perfectly
acceptable in a Marseilles lycée, and a vain boy was naturally
selected as leader of men and arbiter of schoolyard justice.

Social discrimination sometimes set the boarders against the
day boys. A day boy was considered a poor relation. One
particular lout called Pégomas added a sting in the tail, aimed at
Marcel: '. . . and scholarship boys are seedy. The truth is, the
Government makes you have lunch here, because at home
there's nothing to eat.'

Pégomas had the misfortune to be scoffing a croissant at the
time.

> . . . and I was suddenly enflamed with the spitting
> anger of a tomcat. This big bowl of soup had dared to
> mention Joseph's poverty! I took one leap at him, and
> with the bottom of my open palm I struck him under
> the nostrils – with all the force my anger had
> unleashed. It was the Nat Pinkerton blow, which 'dis-
> orientates the enemy'. Mine had a double success, for
> not only had I turned up his nose towards the ceiling
> of the gallery, but my palm, in passing, shoved the

half-eaten croissant, pointed end first, down his windpipe (*Le Temps des Secrets*).

There was no more nonsense from Pégomas, and Marcel was firmly established as a 'formidable fighter and redresser of wrongs'.

Academically, things did not go so well. Marcel was devoured with a sudden appetite for extra-curricular activities like scientific inventions – the internal combustion engine or flying machines – and all kinds of sport. Then he would avidly consume every conceivable literary revue and magazine. Next came opera and theatre. His exam results, especially in Latin, added to Joseph's already considerable worries.

But the gruelling school hours meant Marcel was away from home from seven thirty in the morning until nearly seven at night. He was protected from parental tension as Joseph was occupied giving private tuition and doing the accounts for local shopkeepers to help pay the rent, a constant battle on a schoolmaster's pay.

Parc Borély, a Marseilles park in the fashionable Prado area, where Marcel Pagnol's Tante Rose met her husband-to-be, Oncle Jules, in La Gloire de Mon Père.

Marcel sensibly made use of school rather than school making use of him. He formed a group of close friends, as he would later do with his film crews: Albert Cohen, Yves Bourde, and Fernand Avierinos, sons, respectively, of a Jewish shop-keeper, a merchant seaman who was never at home, and a doctor who provided a sexual education absolutely unavailable from most parents at the time. The inseparable quartet were united in one subject they really liked: French.

Marcel edited a collection of school poems called *The Book of Nature*, twenty of them by himself. Favourite was 'The Song of the Cricket', a hauntingly Provençal sound remembered from sizzling summers in the hills. He also succeeded in finding what every serious student needs: a teacher who respects him. Professor Ripert, himself a poet of some distinction, had taught Latin and French to Edmond Rostand in the same school, and saw in Marcel another poet in the making. Inspired to try his hand at something of the epic proportions of *Cyrano*, Marcel chose Napoleon as his subject. But battles were not his forte. Albert Cohen, his greatest fan, told him his talents were more lyrical than epic. He was a Racine, a Lamartine, an Alfred de Musset.

Marcel was not short on chutzpah. At fifteen, encouraged by Professor Ripert, he started a school magazine, *La Bohème*. After two issues, he decided he was frittering away his talent on a mere school publication and sent a poem entitled 'Summer Night' to the literary revue, *Massilia*, which proceeded to publish a poem signed Marcel Pagnol every month.

At the same time began a rapprochement with the dread Latin. Marcel found in Provençal – a regional, devolutionist language strictly forbidden in school and deplored by Joseph – Latin words and turns of phrase he recognized. It gave him new enthusiasm for Virgil's *Bucolics*; he could identify with the lyrical passages about springs and olive groves, shepherds watching over their flocks beneath silent night skies. Virgil could have been writing about the Provence he so loved.

Euphoria was short lived. That fruitful school year, in which the seeds of Marcel's future were well and truly planted, ended sadly. In June, Augustine died.

He had been especially close to his mother, and had a certain protectiveness towards her. He often felt more like a brother than a son. 'Augustine's age was the same as mine, because my mother was me, and during my childhood I thought we were born the same day' (*La Gloire de Mon Père*).

Her funeral was traumatic.

> . . . I was walking behind a black coach, whose wheels were so tall I could see the horses' shoes. I was dressed in black, and little Paul's hand held mine with all the strength in him. They were taking our mother away for ever.
>
> I have no other memory of that terrible day, as though, at fifteen, I had blocked out the power of a grief that could kill me. Over the years, until we were

grown men, we never had the courage to talk about her.

In this passage from *Le Château de Ma Mère*, published when he was sixty-three, Marcel goes on to talk of the equally premature deaths of brother Paul from epilepsy (in 1932), and his soulmate of summer holidays, Lili des Bellons, killed in action in the First World War.

'Such is the lot of man. A few joys quickly wiped out by unforgettable grief.

You don't have to tell children that.'

Joseph missed Augustine terribly. She had shared his financial worries, and making ends meet may well have been an added burden to her frail health. Now, with four children to feed and René only a few months old, Joseph was faced with the added expense of hiring a governess. Madeleine was pretty and efficient. Two years after Augustine's death Joseph married her, accepting her insistence on the church ceremony he had denied Augustine. To make a few extra francs he even taught English at a private Catholic school. In middle-age he was becoming more humanly pragmatic, less rigid in his socialist, laic beliefs.

Marcel did not notice it. A stepmother was not what an impetuous, self-absorbed teenager needed around the house; nor did he need criticism from a schoolteacher Papa about his education, which was becoming more eclectic every day. A bright Marseillais lycéen naturally devoured Baudelaire's *Fleurs du Mal* and Flaubert's *Madame Bovary*, went to *Manon Lescaut* at the opera, and, with his band of *copains*, surreptitiously sought out the services of a certain Madame who projected flickering images rather more interesting than *The Arrival of the Train at the Station of La Ciotat*.

Though Marseilles was the capital of the pornographic film industry, Marcel never found much joy in it, and his movies, though full of passion and the results of forbidden sex, never showed more than a kiss or, at most, a hand resting motionless upon a thigh. At one of these blue movie sessions, 'before the regrettable closing of houses of tolerance' (in 1946), Marcel encountered a sprightly old *boulevardier* of noble birth.

> I approached the sympathetic gentleman, and as in these places it is the custom to replace ceremony with friendly familiarity, I asked him:
> 'Well, grandpa, are you an old ram?'
> He replied, smiling:

Overleaf: Notre-Dame-de-la-Garde, the nineteenth-century basilica. The monumental statue of the city's patron saint, 'La Bonne Mère', was a landmark for sailors and colonials returning by boat from France's far-flung Empire.

'Young man, you're way off the mark. The only
reason I come to attend these ridiculous frolics is to
thank God I'm no longer in a state to take part' (*Ciné-maturgie de Paris*).

Other sport appealed to Marcel, too. Rather than hanging out
in the smoke and noise of the Café de Bohème, meeting place
of Marseilles youth, he loved cycling in the Parc Borély, sup-
ported Marseilles's first football team, which was composed
entirely of Greeks, and occasionally took part in amateur boxing matches. At one of these, his nose was broken. This added
a certain ruggedness to his dashing looks and later served him
in good stead when filming on location in the tougher corners
of the Old Port; it also made him doubly attractive to women.

In 1913 Marcel was reconciled with his father at a happy
academic event: he had achieved his Baccalauréat in philosophy with an honourable enough mention. Joseph was once
again the proud father, and was even more delighted when
Marcel unhesitatingly opted to follow in Papa's footsteps: a
teacher's life would give him the maximum time for writing.

The reconciliation was short-lived. When choosing between
teacher training colleges at Aix and Marseilles, he opted for the
second, not because it was better but because he was in love
and the girl lived around the corner. She was a pretty brunette,
with green eyes and a Louise Brooks hairstyle, called Simonne
Collin. Her mother – naturally – was a schoolteacher, and Marcel
had known her since she visited their Rue Térrusse apartment,
accompanying her sister for an English lesson from Joseph.

It was all too close for comfort. Even the declaration of war in
1914, when Marcel was just nineteen and too young for call-up,
could not distract him from the yearning of first love.

He and Simonne met every day. A rich friend lent him an
automobile, so the young lovers could drive along the Corniche
to some secluded *calanque*, where they could have rented a
fisherman's hut for a few sous but preferred to make love upon
the luxurious upholstery of a Panhard.

By chance or design – we shall never know – a friend of
Joseph's happened by and saw the young lovers. Moral duty
required that he report the matter to Joseph. Joseph started to
intercept his son's love letters which left him in no doubt about
the state of the affair: Marcel had deflowered a virgin – and
worse, a minor. The wrath of Joseph was terrible. The honour
of the family was at stake. His son would have to marry her.

To an intelligent author, few things are sacred.

Later, in the second act of *Marius*, this incident served the playwright Marcel Pagnol well. Fanny becomes pregnant by Marius, who leaves her holding the baby. Like so many other women abandoned by sailors, Fanny makes her private pilgrimage to the highest point in the city, the hill of Notre-Dame-de-la-Garde. The monumental nineteenth-century church is Marseilles's most famous landmark. Here Fanny prays to the golden Virgin (*La Bonne Mère*), who towers above her on top of the church, to forgive her and bring Marius home safely.

Whenever Marcel Pagnol, as a schoolboy, climbed to this same vantage point, with its magnificent panorama of Marseilles and the Château d'If, he turned his back on the sea. From here he would look longingly eastwards, beyond the city, to the grey, craggy hills where he spent his school holidays.

PAGNOL'S PROVENCE

Those who take the Pagnol trail should not short-change **Marseilles** (see also Chapter IV, pages 91–5). It is an unfairly maligned city that travellers misguidedly bypass – infinitely more interesting than Cannes or Antibes, and these days just as safe, if you take reasonable precautions. Avoid back streets late at night, and the Cours Belsunce at any time. Watch handbags on La Canebière, the main street. Garage your car and walk (easy round the Old Port), or take the Métro or bus.

Marseilles has had a turbulent history, and is justly proud of its independent spirit. In 600 BC the narrow, sheltered bay of Lacydon, where the Old Port now lies, made a perfect harbour for Phocian merchants to establish a Hellenic colony on the shores of Gaul. They came in peace, and their prince, Protis, married the Gallic princess Gyptis. Phocian mariners were the most courageous of the Greeks, and such explorers as Ethymenes made it to the coast of Africa, and Pytheas to the chilly waters of Ultima Thule. Through the waterways of Gaul, the Greeks brought tin from the mines of Cornwall.

The colony of Massilia flourished. During its six centuries, the vine and the olive came to Gaul from Asia Minor, and the new power of the Romans protected it from the Carthaginian general, Hannibal. Gratefully, the Massaliots allowed the Romans to use the city as a naval base. It cost them dearly. In the civil war between Pompey and Julius Caesar in 49 BC, they unfortunately backed the wrong side. Pompey lost, and Julius Caesar deprived Massilia of its precious independence.

Since then, Marseilles has always been fiercely proud of its freedom from any yoke; French kings and Parisian bureau-

Fish soup and vin
rosé *at the Pergola
Restaurant in the
Pagnolian fishing village
of Niolon, just outside
Marseilles.*

cracy were always seen as the heavy hand of interference.

Wisely recognizing its strategic importance as a bastion of naval defence, the bellicose Louis XIV was responsible for reviving the city's fortunes in the seventeenth century. His finance minister, Colbert, squeezed the royal coffers to build not only improved defences at the St-Nicholas fort and the Arsenal, but also the magnificent town hall on the north quay of the Old Port, where Fanny's marriage to Panisse took place.

The Hospice de la Vieille-Charité, one of the most perfectly proportioned buildings still standing in the city, a poorhouse built to cope with the ever-increasing influx of beggars, came under the king's protection in 1689. La Canebière, the wide avenue bisecting the city centre on its way to the Old Port, rivalled the exquisite Cours Mirabeau in Aix, which in turn rivalled the Champs-Élysées. A few kind words from that acerbic letter-writer, the Marquise de Sévigné, were justified: 'I ask Aix's forgiveness, but Marseilles is much prettier and, proportionately, is more heavily populated than Paris. To tell you how many good souls, I did not have the leisure to count. The atmosphere overall there is a little wicked.'

The wickedness of the red light districts behind the port, in the narrow, steep streets of Le Panier and Endoume, pulsating with lubricity and the honky-tonk of mechanical pianos, was far from the Pagnol family's ken. Theirs was a heavily bourgeois Marseilles.

*Opposite: A street in the
Le Panier district of
Marseilles.*

The *quartier* where Marcel spent most of his youth and adolescence is still pleasantly residential. Rue Térrusse is a narrow street of greystone houses with stout grilles protecting ground-floor windows; No.51, the Pagnol home where Augustine died, astonishingly has no commemorative plaque – a first indication of a certain coldness in official Marseilles circles towards the writer for his exuberant and sometimes none-too-flattering portrayal of its citizens. It is the kind of grey street enlivened by prolific window boxes and the sound of a violin being practised by a mercifully professional musician. Round the corner, in the long, straight Boulevard Chave – a typically Mediterranean avenue, with its massive plane trees, reminiscent of Barcelona or Naples – the only trams still functioning emerge from their tunnel under the Place Jean-Jaurez. The tramway was conveniently close to the Pagnols when they set off each summer on their journey up the Huveaune valley to the hills; it makes a brief appearance in the film of *La Gloire de Mon Père*.

On Sunday there's a neighbourhood market in the Place Jean-Jaurez, a square with tall houses shuttered against the morning sun – already dazzling by nine. Provençal dresses, with prints originally imported from India by Marseilles merchants, are displayed in fan shapes. An old carousel gently spins children while their parents shop.

The Lycée Thiers, Marcel's old school, was being renovated when I was there – and not before time. Above it towers the splendid ochre cupola of the Couvent des Bernardins.

Between the Place Jean-Jaurez and the Palais Longchamp is a fine residential area which reflects the fat-cat prosperity of *belle époque* Marseilles. Claude Charles Guillaume Phillipon, a nineteenth-century businessman, gets a whole boulevard named after him; Marcel Pagnol, a twentieth-century author of considerably greater fame, rates a small strip of quayside.

The monumental magnificence of the Palais Longchamp is at its best floodlit. From the top of the ornamental steps of the Gare St-Charles you can share with homing Marseillais, like Marcel returning from Paris, that first view of the city – across the Old Port to Notre-Dame-de-la-Garde. At the Parc Borély, a formal French garden with neatly clipped shrubs and vista to stately château cohabits with a bosky English park – ducks to feed, boats to row, and a rose garden. A sea breeze blows off the ocean to nourish the magnolias, oleanders and palm trees.

Another Sunday treat is the pedestrian precinct at the Canebière end of Rue d'Aubagne, where little Oriental shops sell dried fruit, pistachios, spices, smoked fish and *harissa*. The odours of the Orient, Turkey and Armenia mingle with the Mahgrébin smell of frying *beignets* or wafts of Marseillais pizza.

To see Marseilles's ethnic mix in all its vitality, go to a football match at the Vélodrome on Boulevard Michelet. Supporting Olympique de Marseille, which was started by Marseillais Greeks in 1898, are Kabyle (non-Arabic) Algerians, Tunisian Jews, Vietnamese Catholics, Catalans, Africans, Portuguese, Corsicans, Turks, Armenians and, still, some Greeks. The mighty OM, whatever scandals have surrounded its management in the recent past, is one of the uniting factors of polyglot Marseilles; it is a protector of the city's fragile racial harmony against the racist ravings of the National Front and Jean-Marie Le Pen.

In its painful transition from Port of the Orient to Port of Europe, and for all its unemployment and economic problems, Marseilles still manages to remain the Grand Old Lady of the Mediterranean. A few wrinkles, perhaps, but a great survivor.

For those interested in pursuing Marseilles's history, there are three excellently arranged museums within easy walking distance from the Old Port: Le Jardin des Vestiges (Greek harbour), Les Docks Romains (Roman harbour), and Vieux Marseille (Marseilles at other times).

The residential quarter of Marseilles frequented by the Pagnols does not boast such a variety of hotels and restaurants as the city centre around the Old Port, which will appear in Chapter IV (see pages 91–5). However, for some of the best simple Italian food outside Italy, I recommend Chez Noël at the top end of La Canebière near St-Vincent de Paul church. You'll find out why Marseillais are so proud of their cheese and anchovy pizza in this very friendly establishment.

CHAPTER THREE

HOLIDAYS
IN THE HILLS

*The Huveaune valley, looking towards the
Mediterranean from Marcel Pagnol's
holiday hills.*

*T*he air was calm, and the powerful odours of the hill, like invisible smoke, filled the bottom of the ravine. Thyme, aspic, and rosemary added a green touch to the golden odour of resin whose long, immobile tears were shining on black bark in the limpid shade; I was walking without the least noise in the silence of solitude, when terrifying sounds broke out several paces away from me (*La Gloire de Mon Père*).

Anything could happen. For an adventurous schoolboy like Marcel Pagnol, the hills were a source of constant wonder and excitement. One minute you were walking in silence, the next a rabbit loping through the scrub of the *garrigue* threatened the territory of brightly coloured birds perched on the branches of a dead oak. Their shrieks of protest rent the air and Marcel's hand went instinctively to his hunting-knife. He imagined himself to be a lone Comanche Indian, stalking prey in some wild and dangerous desert, 'dry as Arizona'.

Sophisticated Parisian though Pagnol later became, he was imbued, during these youthful rambles, with a passion for nature, and his accurate evocation of flora and fauna would not have disgraced J. H. Fabre, the great Provençal natural historian. *Baouco*, he tells us, is the yellowy brown grass which resembles dried hay and grows in tufts on the *garrigue*; the Alpine thrush, Corsican blackbird and, of course, the famous *bartavelle* partridge are identified; the turpentine tree, he knows, does not give turpentine oil, and every sort of wild salad is collected. Mention of almond blossom in May when it should be March is a rare lapse; though writing his *Souvenirs d'Enfance* a half-century after the experience, his memory of these 'most beautiful days of my life' was as sharp as his Marseilles wit.

It was a privileged contrast to city life. Whatever privations the Pagnol family suffered at home, Joseph was determined that Augustine, with her weak chest, should breathe cleaner, purer air during the summer holidays. He and Jules together rented a villa at Les Bellons, a hamlet near the hillside village of La Treille, between Marseilles and Aubagne.

The twelve-mile journey took four hours – as long as some Parisians or Londoners now take to reach their Provençal second homes!

The adventure began with the arrival at the Marseilles apartment of François, who spoke only Provençal. This stalwart man of Les Bellons had a *charette bleue*, the traditional blue-painted cart which, for four francs including driver, transported Augustine's pots and pans, Joseph's hunting-gun, provisions, luggage, even the odd bit of furniture to the Quatre-Saisons bar, where the country road bifurcated. Here François would meet them for the last, uphill part of the journey. A place on the cart would be squeezed for Augustine in amongst the Pagnol luggage.

Meanwhile the Pagnols took the tram from the Boulevard Chave tunnel out of the city towards the unaccustomed greenery of the Huveaune valley. The driver allowed Marcel to honk the horn. Forty minutes later they arrived at the village of La Barrasse, the tramway's terminal.

There, Joseph became indignant. Pointing at his map, he showed that their villa was only two and a half miles away as the crow flies. Yet a cluster of châteaux had sealed off richly forested land, necessitating a five-and-a-half-mile detour on foot. Joseph railed against the injustices of private property. 'These walls were not built under the *ancien régime:* not only does our Republic tolerate them, it's even constructed them!'

The detour gave Marcel his first taste of walking in his native countryside. 'The Provençal road was very pretty. It wandered between two walls of stone baked by the sun, over which large leaves of fig trees, and clematis bushes, and hundred-year-old olives leaned towards us.'

The Pagnols were relieved to find François waiting for them at the Quatre-Saisons *buvette*, where thirsty hikers could refresh themselves before attacking the climb. Joseph – usually an amiable, humorous man in spite of his fiercely held convictions – flatly refused to let his family near such a sink of iniquity as a country bar. François drank his pastis alone, while the Pagnols picnicked on crisp, golden bread and white-veined, peppery sausage.

For twenty minutes, the male Pagnols sweated up the dusty, uneven road to La Treille in the July afternoon sun, while Augustine, nursing the two-year-old baby Germaine, lurched perilously on the cart.

> By a supreme effort, we reached the village, or rather the hamlet whose red tiles were the old length. Very small windows pierced thick walls.
>
> To the left was an esplanade bordered with plane trees, supported by a wall sloping backwards, which was at least ten metres high. To the right was the street. I would call it the main street, if there'd been another. But all you encountered was a little cross

street, only ten metres long but even so managing two right-angles before reaching the village square. Smaller than a schoolyard, the little square was shaded by a very old mulberry tree, with a deeply crevassed trunk, and two acacias; in their push to meet the sun, they were trying to beat the belltower.

In the middle of the square, the fountain talked to itself. . .

'The Provençal road was very pretty' – a city boy's first impression of the countryside in La Gloire de Mon Père, *often still as unspoilt as Marcel Pagnol knew it, as here near Riboux (Var), where much of the film* Jean de Florette *was shot.*

They stopped in the village of La Treille for a cautious, city-dweller's drink from the fountain. Water from a reservoir could be, as a local friend later described it, 'essence of frog's piss'. But this was pure, cool fountain water from a spring of the hills – one of those precious springs that would one day inspire Marcel Pagnol to write a screenplay and four hundred pages of fiction. As they drank, Marcel's attention was taken by a giant of a man passing through the tiny square. 'His little eyes shone at the end of a tunnel. A large red moustache covered his mouth, and his cheeks were covered with a week-old beard. Passing by our mule, he spat but didn't say anything. Then, with lowered gaze, he made an uncertain departure.'

The Pagnols knew Provençal country folk could be reserved with strangers – but plain rude? Not all were like that, François explained; this particular man wished him ill, because he was his brother! It was Marcel Pagnol's first experience of another theme which he would later make good use of: the Provençal family feud.

This was the fountain which featured in the 1952 film of

Manon des Sources, where La Treille was the location for the fictitious village of Les Bastides Blanches. Marcel and his wife Jacqueline, who played the first Manon, rented a *belle époque* villa just outside the village, La Pascaline, during the shoot. It was also here that Pagnol, aged sixty-one, began writing the childhood memoirs *Souvenirs d'Enfance* (*La Gloire de Mon Père* and *Le Château de Ma Mère*), which established his literary reputation late in life and were inspired during walks in the *garrigue* and pine woods and wild hills where he spent his childhood holidays.

The steep climb flattened out for a while after the village. A shady avenue of pines led to a turn-off to the even smaller village of Les Bellons. (François was known as François des Bellons, country people often preferring to use the name of the place where the family owned land rather than their family name.) Suddenly the countryside became completely deserted – not a hamlet, not a farm, not even a hut. The road was two dusty ruts, separated by a hump of weeds brushing the belly of the mule. And the hills opened up in all their glory.

François announced their names: La Tête Rouge (the reddish tinge of its conical peak came from a rare limestone, the mauve spots on its side from former bauxite mining), Les Barres de St-Esprit, and Le Garlaban, that distant landmark from Aubagne days which was now a close neighbour. Joseph, with his logical mind, wanted to know why Le Taoumé was also known as Le Tubé. François couldn't tell him – the origins of these names were totally obscure; it just had two names 'like you and me'.

As for Marcel, he had found his El Dorado.

> In front of me, an immense landscape rose in a semi-circle to the sky: black pine woods, separated by little valleys, were about to disappear like waves at the foot of three rocky summits.
>
> Around us, outcrops of lower hills accompanied our road, which snaked along a ridge between two valleys. A great black bird, hovering, marked the middle of the sky, and from all sides, like a sea of music, rose the resounding clamour of cicadas.

Lili des Bellons, son of François, became the city boy's mentor. His real name was David Magnan, but as a baby 'Lili' was as close as he could get to pronouncing David. Nine-year-old Marcel immediately began learning from Lili's atavistic knowledge of these hills and their nature, though he was two years younger. Lili had style.

He wore, under an old grey wool waistcoat, a brown shirt with long sleeves rolled up to the elbows, short pants, and rope espadrilles like mine, only with socks.

'When you find game in a trap,' he said, 'you're allowed to take it, but you must reset the trap, and put it back in place' (*Le Château de Ma Mère*).

Childhood friends: country boy Lili des Bellons (Joris Molinas) teaches city boy Marcel Pagnol (Julien Ciamaca) how to smoke dry clematis in Yves Robert's film of La Gloire de Mon Père *(1990).*

Hunter's law, and Marcel soon learned to obey it when trapping with Lili. He also learned from his new friend the Provençal names: *bedouïdes* were larks, *darnagas* shrikes, *limberts* lizards. Lili helped him to identify wild salad, morel mushrooms, arbutus that you never saw in a Marseilles schoolyard and, even less, rue – a herb eaten instinctively by a ewe to abort a malformed lamb and by village girls in trouble.

Lili and Marcel were near neighbours. Lili was born in a handsome bastide which still stands at the end of an alley of trim box hedge. The Pagnols' holiday villa, last house on the road a little higher up, was called La Bastide Neuve. It had been 'new' for a very long time – a small ruined farmhouse, restored some thirty years previously by a Marseillais.

Comfort was sacrificed for ambience. Apart from its Water Tap of Progress, a brass tap which ended the pipe's run from the water cistern to the kitchen sink, there was no modern amenity. Toilets were outside and showers provided by a hose. The garden seemed to Marcel like a virgin forest of olive and almond trees, and a vast fig tree on the terrace was their summer dining room. And with the heady holiday mood, Joseph allowed himself the occasional glass of Oncle Jules's wine.

Wine, according to Jean Giono, has been used for shaving in a Midi drought, but the abstemious Joseph never had to face the horror of what it might do to his skin, let alone his conscience. He shaved, with Oncle Jules, under the fig tree just as he did in Marseilles. The running water at La Bastide Neuve was a rare luxury in those parched highlands. Marcel came to know it as 'the country of thirst'. From the village fountain to the summits of the Étoile range, there were only a dozen or so wells spread over twelve miles. Most of these were dry by May. François told Joseph that he never went to Mass to pray for a drought to end. Only when it rained. 'We have to make the Good Lord understand,' he said.

Joseph, facts always at his fingertips, pronounced that the annual rainfall of Paris was forty-five centimetres, whereas Marseilles had sixty centimetres. How could so much rain disappear, even in these rocky limestone hills? Underground streams, fed from the plateaux, must emerge somewhere in the valleys, in caves, dripping into moss from cracks in the rocks. There must be more than the three or four springs on the map.

Lili knew of seven such springs. Much as he liked the Pagnols, he would not divulge where they were. You never revealed such things. The villagers of Allauch or Peypin might get to know; they might want to drink the water. Or day trippers might find the springs. Cool water incited hot emotions in these hills. That's why the springs had to be kept secret.

Sometimes this secrecy could backfire.

Lili's grandfather knew of a spring he wouldn't even tell his own family about. On his deathbed he began to reveal the secret of its whereabouts to Lili's father, croaking: 'François, François, the spring . . . the spring . . .' They were the last words he spoke.

Much later in life, Marcel Pagnol was to put 'the country of thirst' and its feuds to good account in *Jean de Florette* and *Manon des Sources*.

Marcel also experienced, for the first time, the joy of summer eating, al fresco, beneath their shady fig tree. Augustine's cooking had never been so aromatic and appetizing. He brought his mother prickly bouquets of thyme, fresh from the *garrigue*, which was impregnated with its Virgilian perfume. François introduced her to *pèbre d'aï* (donkey's pepper – an aphrodisiac, but not only for donkeys), as an even better flavouring for a rabbit stew. Its flavour was somewhere between mint and thyme, he said. The French call it *sariette* (savoury).

Marcel loved the stew's dark, velvety sauce. He would look around for the liver, his favourite. Then, teasingly, Oncle Jules would plunge his fork into it, saying: 'Admirably cooked . . . tender, juicy. . . I would feel obliged to offer it to someone, if at this table there wasn't a certain person who believes it to be poisoned!' And, with loud sarcastic laughter, he popped it into his own mouth. Oncle Jules had a sense of humour which Marcel appreciated a good deal less than his mother's cooking. There were bacon omelettes and stuffed tomatoes and green olives from their own trees, preserved in brine in earthenware jars, and all kinds of mushrooms you really had to know your way about or die. There was apricot tart, made of the freshest fruit, or Marcel could just reach up during dinner and pick fresh figs for dessert from their own tree.

Lighting came from an oil hurricane lamp, and the insects came with it. 'As soon as it was hung on its branch, it was surrounded by a flight of plump moths whose shadows danced on the tablecloth: burned by impossible love, they fell perfectly cooked on to our plates' (*La Gloire de Mon Père*). Giant wasps had the family flapping madly with their napkins, occasionally knocking over a carafe of precious water or smashing a glass.

Joseph was eager that Marcel and Paul should be *au fait* with the small wildlife around them, both as insectologists and for self-preservation. Vicious everyday insects, like hornets and scorpions, are strangely not mentioned. Instead, the boys studied industrious ants at work in the *baouco*. They discovered the Provençal name *prégadiou* (prie-dieu or praying-chair) for a praying mantis. With laic relish, Joseph warned them that in spite of its religious name it was the tiger of insects and would eat grasshoppers and even butterflies alive. Later, Marcel Pagnol used the surreal, tongue-rolling Provençal insult '*prégadiou de rastouble*' (praying mantis of straw) in *Jofroi*, where it is delivered by an old peasant to a priest.

An old peasant also taught Marcel and Paul how to catch cicadas on the bark of olive trees. Paul stuffed them in every available pocket, and they would surprise the family by bursting into song at dinner.

Preparation for the hunting season was the main topic of conversation between their father and uncle. So far Oncle Jules had only been after small game; the usual August storms had brought rain and, with it, snails. He came back soaked but happy, his salad basket full, with snails on his shoulders like epaulettes and the enormous 'tribe's chieftain' indignantly showing its horns.

Opposite: La Bastide Neuve, the Pagnol holiday home near La Treille. Marcel Pagnol only ever succeeded in persuading its peasant owner to sell this half of it.

My father's glory: Joseph Pagnol (Philippe Caubère), Marcel's father, going hunting with Oncle Jules (Didier Pain) on the day of his bagging a brace of bartavelles *in* La Gloire de Mon Père *(1990).*

Now it was time for the serious stuff. A most unappetizing smell of cooking came from kitchen. It was Oncle Jules 'frying' shot for his cartridges, which he resolutely filled himself. Joseph was, for once, the pupil. 'My father, child of the city and prisoner of schools, had killed neither fur nor feather. But Oncle Jules had hunted since childhood, and made no secret of it.' Patronizingly, he inspected Joseph's second-hand gun and declared it an 'arquebus' – a little large for some of the game. Peasants, he declared, popped off at anything that moved, apart from canaries and parrots: thrushes, buntings and red partridges; rabbits and hares; woodcock and wild boar. But what, he asked Joseph, was the King of Game, the hunter's dream trophy?

Paul guessed elephants. Wrong. Joseph guessed pheasants. Wrong again. It was, of course, the famous *bartavelle*, the royal partridge which lived on the heights above rocky valleys and was as wary as a fox.

The hunting season opened, but not one local hunter from La Treille or Les Bellons, nor even poachers from Allauch and Peypin, could be seen. They always avoided the first day: gendarmes were thick on the ground, checking permits. Joseph and Oncle Jules had the good game preserves to themselves from the Vallon des Escaouprès to the Puits du Mûrier.

Marcel was worried. Would Joseph, champion of *boules*, make a fool of himself at this new sport? 'Would he return with an empty game bag, while Oncle Jules laid out partridges and hares as though dressing a shop window? No, no! That couldn't happen: I would follow all day and put up birds, and rabbits, and hares, so he'd end up actually killing one.'

Oncle Jules was as intolerant of Joseph's clumsy misses as he was generous about his final triumph. For towards the end of the day's hunting, Joseph had a stroke of beginner's luck: a left and right barrel, two birds ... and no ordinary birds either. . .

It was Marcel who found them. Proudly, he called down from a rock high above the hunters. 'And in my small, bloody fists from which four golden wings hung, towards the sky I raised the glory of my father in the setting sun.'

Not one, but two *bartavelles*! Joseph was suddenly the most famous man in La Treille. Even the Curé, whom Joseph had greeted coolly in the *boulangerie*, won him over by ornithological erudition. The Curé turned out to be a royal partridge buff. 'You have there an old male and a ten-year-old hen. My father was a great hunter, and that's how I know so much. This partridge is not the *Caccabis rufa*, which is much smaller. It is the *Caccabis saxatilis*, or rock partridge, which one also calls the Greek partridge, and in Provence the *bartavelle*.'

Considering Joseph to have been blessed by St-Hubert, patron saint of hunters, the Curé offered another favour. He was also a camera buff, and immortalized Joseph's glory with a photograph. Vanity was, after all, not a mortal sin.

On that solo trek, following the hunters, Marcel had his first real taste of the hills. He seemed to be walking on one immense bluish, chalky flagstone. The escarpments sprouted little pine trees from their sheer sides. There were mysterious caves to be explored. On the arid plateau, nothing grew but kermes-oak, rosemary, and lavender. Pines with gnarled trunks were bent by the mistral. You could walk for twenty miles up there and see no buildings but ruined medieval farms and abandoned sheepfolds.

He made the hills his own – and so did his family, especially his younger brother, Paul, who suffered from epilepsy. Humiliated by the fits which afflicted him in public, Paul retreated from the world to become the last goatherd in the Massif de L'Étoile. He slept rough, preferring the stars above him to a claustrophobic roof. He played the harmonica – like Manon and her father, Jean de Florette. In the preface to his translation of Virgil's *Bucolics,* Marcel writes fondly of his brother: 'He played ancient little melodies, belonging to the paths of Étoile, Sainte-Baume or Gineste, which had come to him from the depths of time.'

A Shepherd's Stone near the ruined sheepfold Jas de Baptiste is carved with a rosette, a serpent, a hand and a flower,

probably to ward off evil spirits. These heights were pagan and
mysterious and Marcel found himself drawn back to them again
and again.

> The powerful July sun started the cicadas chirruping;
> on the edge of the mule track, spiders' webs glistened
> among the genista bushes. Climbing slowly towards
> the Jas de Baptiste, my sandals found the footsteps of
> last year, and the landscape recognized me. . .
>
> When I arrived at the foot of Le Taoumé's big top,
> I sat under the huge, bent pine tree, and contem-
> plated the countryside for a long time.
>
> Far, far to my right, beyond lower hills, the morn-
> ing sea sparkled. . .
>
> A light breeze had just risen: suddenly, it stirred up
> the perfume of thyme and lavender. Leaning back on
> my hands, with eyes closed, I breathed the burning
> fragrance of my country. . . (*Le Temps des Secrets*).

Thanks to Lili, Marcel continued to become more know-
ledgeable about the hills. They were inseparable adventurers.
Lili had game-traps everywhere. He said you couldn't be fussy
about what you ate in the country. Lizard was tasty, and a lot
better than snake. He preferred badger to fox which, for his
personal taste, had too strong a smell. In his time, he'd eaten
just about everything, including hedgehogs. What was so odd
about that? People ate sea-urchins, didn't they? And there were
even filthy beasts who ate frogs!

Marcel was glad of a proper French picnic. His mother filled
his backpack with bread, butter, sausage, pâté, two lamb chops,
and four bananas.

In those days there were no fire regulations to impede their
cook-outs. 'Over a crackling braise of myrtle and rosemary, Lili
set up a square grill he'd brought with him for my cutlets and
three sausages. . . They wept sizzling tears of fat, and the heavy,
appetizing smoke made my mouth water like a young dog.'

Dessert grew wild. Lili knew of a secret thicket where long-
forgotten vines, spared by phylloxera, still provided tart but
delicious grapes. To round the feast off he would cut a branch
of dry clematis, slice a length between the knots and, thanks to
the thousand invisible channels which ran along the warp of
the wood, it could be smoked like a cigar.

He took Marcel to La Chantepierre, a little pinnacle of rock
pierced with holes, which made it sing in the wind. When rain
approached 'an old, very sad hunting horn sounded in the

depths of a damp forest'. The mistral produced a yowling cat. Of the thirty-seven Provençal winds, one called the 'Spinsters' Wind' produced a whole ladies' choir giving genteel voice. 'Then a glass flute . . . way up in the clouds, accompanied the voice of a small girl singing on the banks of a stream' (*Le Château de Ma Mère*).

Marcel's flights of poetic imagination were sometimes grounded by the harsh reality of the hills. Once, he and Lili were caught in a memorable storm. Lili knew it would rain. 'If you had to drink all the water that's going to fall, you'd pee till Christmas,' he said. Beneath violet clouds, the bluish light got darker and darker over the Vallon du Jardinier and the rocky sides of the Gorges de Passe-Temps. They were hurrying to the slopes of Le Taoumé to collect game from their traps before the storm broke. In the awful stillness, the cries of uneasy animals could be heard. Then a distant rumble. The first, huge drops of rain fell on the grey rock. 'Then, suddenly a quick flash of lightning, followed by a dry, vibrating thunderbolt, split the clouds which dissolved in an immense pattering on the *garrigue*.'

And Lili also dissolved – in uproarious laughter. Bravado, perhaps. Marcel saw he was pale, and Marcel felt pale too. Lili knew where to find shelter, though: a poachers' cave near the top of Le Taoumé, a narrow tunnel with a hole in the escarpments on either side of the peak – useful when a poacher was on the run from the gendarmes: he could exit or enter in either direction. From here, the friends had a grandstand view of the gods' wrath. 'We were perfectly sheltered and just cocking a snook at the full force of the storm, when a bloodthirsty, screaming thunderbolt struck a long hill quite close to us, causing a whole slab of rock to fall.'

La Grotte du Grosibou, where Marcel and Lili encountered the Grand Duke.

Then Lili became aware they were not alone. But it wasn't a poacher behind them in the cave, nor a gendarme looking for one. Lili told Marcel to turn, ever so slowly. In the darkness of the cave, Marcel saw two piercing eyes. They were not human. A vampire?

It was the Grand Duke, the big owl of Provence.

'"If he attacks us, watch out for your eyes!" Lili whispered.

'Terror suddenly took me over.

'"Let's go," I said, "let's go! Better to be wet than blind."'

And they made a dash for it, like two poachers on the run from the gendarmes, back to La Bastide Neuve and a good, hot fire in the marble chimney to warm themselves.

As the villa was rented by the year, the Pagnols had enough experience of its cosy possibilities to decide to come for Christmas. 'In a sky of violet velvet, innumerable stars shone. They were no longer the gentle stars of summer. They glittered hard, clear and cold, crystallized by the night frost. . .' The Christmas tree, the Provençal 'thirteen desserts' at the réveillon supper, crisp air and clear views made the season particularly festive. Joseph, since his friendship with the Curé, even forgave Oncle Jules for celebrating Midnight Mass in La Treille, and Oncle Jules prayed that he might one day be converted to the Faith.

Augustine had a more practical idea. Christmas had been such a success, why didn't they come for weekends too? Everyone agreed it was a good idea. But there was the problem of a four-hour journey each way on a schoolmaster's weekend: a short cut was the solution.

On one of their journeys, they had encountered an old pupil of Joseph's, Bouzigue. Bouzigue was now keeper of the narrow canal which linked the grounds of those four châteaux whose very existence made Joseph see the red of the silk tie he wore on Bastille Day. The loyal Bouzigue, grateful for good exam results, offered Joseph the key to the gates. The canal path ended near the Quatre-Saisons *buvette*, cutting down the road's long loop to a mere thirty minutes.

As an honest servant of the French Republic, Joseph was worried by the legality of it – even accompanied, on the first walk, by Bouzigue. For Marcel and Paul, it was a walk through an enchanted forest. As the limpid water followed its straight and narrow course on their left, on their right were the gardens of the châteaux, separated by gates along the canal path. Clematis, rosemary, fennel, and cistus grew in jungly abandon; their roots, Bouzigue explained, held the earth of the banks firm, and the châteaux owners were forbidden to cut them back.

The first château – turreted, with vines and meadows around its terrace – belonged to a sick count, who was looked after by a genial manservant. No problem there. Then came the Sleeping Beauty's Château, with shutters closed, surrounded by abandoned fields and hundred-year-old pines. No problem there, either. Then came the Notary's Château, an August holiday home occupied for the rest of the year only by a senile grandfather. Still no problem. And finally, the fourth château – the most impressive in size and splendour – owned by an absentee Parisian. His caretaker was a drunk with a bad leg and a twenty-year-old, one-eyed dog that could hardly move.

There certainly seemed no live impediment to the Pagnol's trespassing. And, the meticulous Joseph observed, they had done in twenty-four minutes flat what normally took them two hours forty-five minutes. After a moment's wrestling with his over-developed conscience, Joseph took the key from Bouzigue, warning his family that he was not at all certain that he would make use of it next Saturday.

But he did. Marcel led the way, and would signal danger. There was none. The kindly Bouzigue, they discovered, had warned the sick count's manservant who had, in turn, warned the count, who had risen from his sick bed to greet them. Joseph was forced to re-evaluate both the aristocracy and the military. The count had once been a colonel, and preferred to be known as such. The colonel (a touching cameo by the great actor, Georges Wilson, in the film of *Le Château de Ma Mère*), who had fought in the Franco-Prussian War, kissed Augustine's hand and presented her with bouquets of red roses picked by himself; his manservant – a uniformed giant called Vladimir – romped with the children; and the Pagnols were regularly invited to a sumptuous tea on the terrace. If Bouzigue was regularly referred to as 'Boutique' by the colonel, they had to make allowances.

Their reception at the fourth château was less cordial. Augustine always became nervous as they approached it; her woman's intuition told her that the mean caretaker had been spying on them. One terrible Saturday she was proved right: Joseph, brandishing his key, found the last gate, which led to the road and safety, firmly secured with a padlock and chain.

In a flash the caretaker (another fine cameo performance by the late Jean Carmet) was upon them, hurling drunken insults. Who did they think they were, trespassing on Monsieur le Baron's property? A schoolteacher? Where were his papers? Joseph, eager to prove himself no liar, produced his ID. The caretaker immediately confiscated it, together with the key.

Meanwhile, the twenty-year-old, one-eyed mutt seemed hungry to prove that there was life in the old guard dog yet; he snarled and panted on his leash. The caretaker had the Pagnols unpack all their belongings, even down to a harmless alarm clock, on the pretext of searching for stolen goods.

> At that moment, the bell of the alarm clock went off like a firework: my mother, letting out a cry, collapsed on to the grass. I rushed forwards; she fainted in my arms. The caretaker, who was at the bottom of the bank, turned and took in the scene. He began to laugh, and said jovially:
> 'Good try, but it won't work!'

The Pagnols had to retrace their footsteps. And, worse, Joseph no longer had the key for the other gates. Adding to his growing crime record, he was forced to steal a length of wire from a vine support and pick the locks like a common thief. The journey to La Bastide Neuve that day took five hours, maybe six – nobody had thought to time it. Moreover, Joseph would doubtless be reported by the caretaker and would lose his job.

The resourceful Bouzigue came to the rescue. It was a question of *jouer le piston*, using his influence. Did he not have a sister who had compromised a Préfet of Marseilles by taking photographs of the two of them in bed together? Could he not equally compromise the caretaker by threatening him with legal proceedings for illegally putting a chain and padlock on a gate used by the canal-keeper? Bouzigue, with a posse of strong-armed colleagues, traded Joseph's confiscated papers for dropping the legal proceedings. And yet another Pagnol story ended happily.

A couple of adventures in the hills were less successful, however. There was the time Marcel decided to become a hermit. He could perfectly well, he decided, live on wild asparagus, chick peas, snails, and sloes. He would sleep in a cave on a bed of *baouco*. He would wash . . . then Lili showed him how and where he would wash, if at all, in a handful of spring water. No soap, no hot water. In winter?! Then Lili told him about the ghost of Félix the shepherd who roamed the hills at night. . .

That did it. Marcel's one night on the dark mountain was over. '. . . the dawn pierced the pale mist: in a diffuse light, little cotton clouds remained hanging on the branches of pine trees and on the tips of brushwood. It was cold' (*Le Château de Ma*

Les Barres de St-Esprit, the hill that was later part of location land owned by Marcel Pagnol, where a Provençal village was constructed for the film of Regain. *It confused airline pilots, who could not find it on the map.*

Mère). He was back in bed at La Bastide Neuve long before his parents could find his farewell note.

The adventure with Isabelle lasted longer.

Marcel met her while out collecting thyme for his mother in the Vallon de Rapon. This was one of his magic places, its silence pervasive, where 'rough peasants long ago cultivated their vines, buckwheat, and chick peas'. Now it was overgrown with fennel, giving out a pungent odour of *anis* as Marcel, using his stick and knife, ploughed his way through.

And there, terrified by a huge spider's web which blocked her path, was a girl like no other he had ever seen. 'On long curls of shining black, she wore a crown of daisies, and she clasped to her breast an armful of white clematis, mixed with wild irises and foxgloves' (*Le Temps des Secrets*).

It was, if not love, infatuation at first sight. She made him blush, and that infuriated an eleven-year-old so sure of himself in other ways.

Isabelle turned out to be the girl nearly next door at Les Bellons. Same age, different class. She lived in the biggest house in the village and called the *salon* by the affected Franglais word '*livigroub*' – 'living-room' with a bad cold. Her mother, a professor of music, addressed her as *vous*, never *tu*, as nobles did their closest family. Her father was the flamboyant, absinthe-drinking poet, Loïs de Montmajour. His poems were published in a Paris revue, Isabelle boasted to Marcel.

Late with the thyme for his mother's rabbit stew, Marcel excused himself for spoiling the lunch: he had been rescuing a damsel in distress.

First love: when out gathering thyme for his mother's stew, Marcel meets Isabelle, later to become his 'Red Queen' in Yves Robert's film of Le Château de Ma Mère *(1990).*

The family was unimpressed – especially Oncle Jules, who had never heard of Loïs de Montmajour, let alone read his poems. Paris was a long way away, he said. And imagine the stunned silence when Marcel informed Joseph and Oncle Jules, those intrepid hunters, that the Montmajours would rather kill hunters than game. Marcel was blind to their preciousness. It even rubbed off on him. He became Isabelle's slave and spent every spare minute in her company. She replaced Lili in his affections, though Lili wisely warned him that 'a friend is not a slave'.

He was impressed by the ambience which Isabelle's father worked hard at – a provincial cross between Gabriele d'Annunzio and Stéphane Mallarmé, decadent and symbolist. His poetry readings by candlelight and his absinthe-drinking were ceremonies, and he called his wife: 'My Infanta!' 'His poems were all in the same vein. There were blind kings who wept at the feet of mad queens, lame dwarfs who hopped, sneering, about the crenallations of the tower. . .'

In this heady atmosphere, Isabelle suggested they play the game of the Queen and her Knight. Her dress had a long, scarlet train, her sceptre was red, and he called her the Red Queen; he wore a fireman's helmet with a feather stuck in it and brandished a wooden sword.

The Red Queen set her Knight various labours to prove his love: he must climb to the highest branch of a prickly acacia to bring her an abandoned bird's nest; he must descend to the bottom of a well and retrieve a rose; he must tame a vicious, starving farm dog. The Red Queen was pleased with her Knight. She gave him his reward. He closed his eyes and opened his mouth for a caramel, a cherry . . . a slug. And then the games ended.

One day Marcel arrived chez Montmajour to a scene of disarray. The house seemed deserted. A strong smell of cat shit had replaced the sweet odour of *anis* in the '*livigroub*'. The table was a mess of uncleared dishes and guttered candles. And to the banal din of a flushing toilet, his Red Queen made her appearance. She was sick to her stomach, she said, and the cat had 'done horrors in the corners'. Everyone was sick.

To make matters worse, Marcel spotted an exercise book marked 'Isabelle Cassignol' and a letter addressed to 'Adolphe Cassignol, Proof Reader of *Le Petit Marseillais*'. Who was Loïs de Montmajour? Answer: a pretentious pseudonym for a boozy Marseilles newspaper employee to impress the peasants of Les Bellons.

First love ended abruptly for Marcel. Lili forgave his temporary desertion and the two of them watched the departure of Isabelle Cassignol and her drunken father for Marseilles. Marcel was filled with melancholy. The holidays, like first love, had come to an end.

In the distance, an enormous red sun was sinking into a sulphur sea, our shadows were already long. . .

The first breaths of evening, barely perceptible, were hurrying towards us from the top of the slopes. In the sky, a black flight of starlings dived and climbed . . . then, across the resinous silence of the pine woods, a few lost notes of the angelus in Allauch echoed through the long hills, spreading the good word. . .

In my night dreams, I heard distant music, and the little Red Queen faded away, infinitely sad and alone, into the twilit arches of a forest of long ago.

PAGNOL'S PROVENCE

Happily, a light mistral was blowing in a cloudless sky as we headed for the hills from **Aubagne**. March was the perfect month – clear visibility for the views, a cool breeze for the thirteen-mile trek. In the hottest months, July and August, the hills are closed to tourists because of fire hazard. The Tourist Board was helpful in providing maps and guides, showing the sites familiar to us by now from Pagnol's books and films – La Bastide Neuve, Lili's house, the Cave of the Big Owl, and the Garlaban with its tump-topped, 2,328-foot summit dominating Aubagne.

Paths are often stony; bring good walking shoes and a light picnic – plus water, if you don't trust lowering an old Évian bottle on a string into a well. You also need to keep your eyes skinned for the guiding initials MP on rocks along the trail.

Our start was a short drive out of town. Very soon after leaving Aubagne on the badly signposted road to Eoures, the urban sprawl diminished. Little vineyards and orchards began to separate the houses. To the right, as the narrow road wound upwards, the foothills of Pagnolia announced themselves with Aleppo pines hovering over neat gardens. And above us, beyond the houses, the bare slopes of the Massif de L'Étoile opened up their *garrigue* wildness to a cloudless blue. Here was coastal countryside without acres of industrial greenhouses.

A number of choices must now be made by the trekker. There are two circuits, one thirteen miles long, the other six. They can be walked in either direction. Both circuits, however, are horseshoe-shaped, ending and beginning some four miles apart. To avoid the extra walk back to your car on a boring, busy road, you leave it in a car park either at La Treille or at La Ferme d'Angèle restaurant, and pick up a local bus (running roughly every two hours) for the ten-minute ride to your chosen starting point.

La Treille remains low-key for a literary shrine. No Marcel Pagnol pizzerias or Jean de Florette crêperies. There isn't even a *boulanger*, let alone his *femme*. With no unsightly modern buildings and a healthily unrestored look, La Treille astonishingly lies in the eleventh arrondissement of Marseilles. Apart from Manon's fountain, there's the esplanade where *Jofroi* was shot, and another Pagnol location, the Cigalon restaurant, where a reasonable meal can be had. At the bottom of the town is the cemetery where Marcel Pagnol and many of his family are buried (see Chapter VI, page 138).

Pagnol never managed to buy the whole of **La Bastide Neuve**, just half of it. The other half is a *buvette* where trekkers can get refreshing soft drinks in 'the land of thirst'. *Bastide* is a Midi word for country house, used very loosely. It really means a fortified farm, but a Marseillais may call his shooting-hut a *bastide*; and a pretentious marquis, like the squire in *La Femme du Boulanger*, may add castellations to his genuine *bastide* and call it a château. Midi houses are still status symbols, and the one-upmanship of second-home owners continues to blight the area.

The present owners of La Bastide Neuve have kept the famous fig tree. Sadly missing, however, is the outside WC, the little hut where Joseph and Oncle Jules prepared for the hunting season by a little target practice against the door. They had not realized that the daily maid, glad of such a luxury, was in there making use of it. While they reloaded, she cautiously opened the door to ask, 'Can I come out now?'

Continuing the bracing climb into the wilderness, we found Marcel's *garrigue* still retained its sweet-scented solitude, the hills their plant and insect life. Spanish lilac, cistus, genista, hellebore and box grow in profusion. Certain places are known for certain plants – the Vallon d'Escaouprès for *pèbre d'aï*, the hillside of Le Taoumé for lavender, La Baume Sourne for morels. In spring, ladybirds huddle together in hundreds after

La Baume Sourne, one of Marcel Pagnol's favourite caves, today a cool stopping-place for a picnic on the 13-mile walk in the L'Étoile hills.

wintering in thick gorse bushes, then fly way down to the blossoming rose bushes of Marseilles villas.

From a rest stop between the **Jas de Baptiste** sheepfold and the **Shepherd's Stone**, we were treated to a breathtaking panorama of the whole city of Marseilles – from L'Estaque to Montredon. Silhouetted against a glistening Mediterranean was the church of Notre-Dame-de-la-Garde on its hill above the Old Port. It is the highest point in the city, from where the young Marcel would look longingly out towards these windswept, sun-drenched hills, as though to reassure himself that they were still there.

After slithering sideways (not for the overweight, this) through the narrow entrance of **La Grotte du Grosibou**, where no Grand Duke Owl greeted us, we headed for the summit of **Le Taoumé**. Though only 2,196 feet high, it seemed like the top of the world. Inland, a vast panoramic sweep – the snow-covered Alps above Digne to the right and the lone hump of Mont Ventoux to the left. The latter is about fifty miles away. Highest point is **Le Plan de l'Aigle** (2,394 feet). It is a rocky mesa supplying a perfect spot for Thompson's car-phone transmitters, some half-dozen pylons marring the natural beauty. Cézanne would have hated the eyesore; his Montagne Ste-Victoire is yet another landmark to be seen from these prolific heights.

Even a ten-minute detour to the tump top of **Garlaban** does not take you higher than the deceptive Plan de l'Aigle. From its *table d'orientation* by an iron cross, when a mistral sweeps the horizon clear, there is another magnificent view to the Chaîne de Mont Carpiagne coastal range and Cap Canaille, the highest cliff in Europe (1,027 feet), with a glimmer of sea beyond.

A pleasant picnic spot has been arranged for today's trekkers at **La Baume Sourne**. Before May, when the wells dry up, water can be had by lowering a bottle into the nearby **Puits du Mûrier**. A track leads down from the fire-road that runs along the crest north of Le Taoumé. La Baume Sourne is another cave, with shady sumac trees near by. Now the rocky descent begins, past Garlaban, **Manon's Cave** and **Les Barres de St-Esprit**. The film locations here belong to other chapters (see pages 138 and 119).

As for the **Château de la Buzine**, it is now a sorry sight, only just qualifying as a romantic ruin because of its associations. It is also hard to find. Persevering Pagnolians, taking the D2 (towards Aubagne), turn left at the roundabout marked to Parc des Sept Collines. The château is about half a mile on the right.

Visible from a cemetery on the Marseilles-Aubagne main road

is the turreted Second Empire **Sleeping Beauty's Château** (Régis) and, further towards Aubagne, the sixteenth-century **Notary's Château** (La Reynarde). Take a helicopter ride and you'll discover these are not strictly linked by the famous canal. Even Marcel Pagnol took poetic licence.

Where to stay and eat: at Gémenos (see the suggestions given in Chapter I, page 27). For those with a hearty appetite after a thirteen-mile trek, there is also the Ferme d'Angèle restaurant (moderate) near the Ruissatel car park, and Le Cigalon (inexpensive) at La Treille.

CHAPTER FOUR

THE
OLD PORT

*Vallon des Auffes, a Pagnolian creek on the
Marseilles Corniche, with good, atmospheric
restaurants for* bouillabaisse *and other
seafood specialities.*

*M*arius left Fanny in the Old Port of Marseilles to see the world, not on some footloose whim but to fulfil his destiny. The maritime Greeks of Lacydon, as much as the playwrights of Athens, had natural inheritors in Marius and his creator, Marcel Pagnol. In his restless teens, Pagnol must have felt the same longing to be 'somewhere else'. However, there was no question of him deserting his girlfriend, Simonne, as Marius did Fanny. The little Red Queen of those holidays in the hills may have been first love without sex, but Simonne was first sex with love.

Joseph, his father, insisted on marriage. The Pagnols lived far from the maritime morals of the Old Port, and a girl whose virginity you took you married, even if she was not pregnant. Family honour was at stake.

In 1916 Marcel and Simonne were married at the town hall on the Quai du Port, like Panisse and Fanny in *The Marseilles Trilogy*. Marcel was twenty-one.

The years of struggle to come, accompanied by the loyal Simonne, could hardly be called destiny-fulfilling. But they paid the rent. In other respects, they were a baptism of fire which served him far better than First World War trenches. The death of his friend, Lili des Bellons, aged nineteen, only confirmed his anti-militarism. After brief service in the quartermaster stores in Nice, Marcel was invalided out for 'feebleness of constitution'. For a young man who had had his nose broken boxing and whose childhood holidays were spent trekking in rocky hills, 'feebleness of constitution' could only be read as 'sheer boredom' plus the Good Soldier Schweik's ability to con the medical authorities.

Anyway, it left Marcel free to pursue his teaching career, and his writing. He certainly got around, if not, like Marius, to faraway places with strange-sounding names ('Suez, Aden, Bombay, Madras, Colombo, Macassar'), at least to schools in towns that were a change from Marseilles. One can imagine a Hollywood bio-pic, with names of places dissolving over pounding pistons and turning train wheels, a montage of different classrooms, each school a promotion in his rise to academic success.

Tarascon . . Digne . . . Pamiers-sur-Arièges. . .

Tarascon, a fine medieval town on the borders of Provence and the Languedoc, is separated from its sister-town of Beaucaire by the wide-flowing Rhône. More interesting to Marcel than its castle was its setting for Alphonse Daudet's *Tartarin de Tarascon*. Digne was also pleasant enough – a spa town in the Alps of High Provence, fresh and bracing for a budding writer's brain. But Pamiers-sur-Arièges? Promotion? It was a one-bar village in the Pyrenees. Simonne was homesick for Marseilles. Marcel was despised for not being at the Front. They were both ill from undernourishment.

Pamiers-sur-Arièges . . . Aix-en-Provence . . . Marseilles. . . Aix has the Cours Mirabeau, that most elegant of main streets, where the Deux Garçons café is the perfect place for a young writer to scribble his notes on a serviette. And Marcel taught at the Lycée Mignet, where Zola and Cézanne had been schoolfriends. Marseilles had him as master at the St-Charles, an annexe of his old school, the Lycée Thiers. And from there. . .

PARIS!

In 1922 he was appointed to the Lycée Condorcet, Paris, as Assistant Professor of English. Dickens and Shakespeare were added to the Graeco-Roman influence of Virgil and Catullus, and Pagnol's copious reading and writing had prepared him well for the exigent Paris literary scene, where quotations were bandied about like smalltalk.

From the age of nineteen, Pagnol had created and directed a Marseilles literary magazine, *Fortunio*, which was closed down by the war. While teaching at Aix-en-Provence after the Armistice, he revived it and now became its Paris editor in a retitled version, *Cahiers du Sud*. Its aim was to bring Marseilles poetry to the capital. Though dogged by squabbles and petty jealousy of Pagnol for his business sense and push, the magazine was just the entrée to the literary world Pagnol needed. A struggling writer from the provinces had to have more than driving ambition and talent; without contacts, he was nowhere. He met theatre people like the impresarios, Léon and Simone Volterra, who eventually put on *Marius*, his first big hit with a Provençal setting.

Parisians loved Pagnol's Marseilles accent. They were charmed by his meridional looks. They sat back and waited.

In the twenties, when competition in every field of Parisian art was a dogfight of egos, it took Pagnol a tough five years to emerge on top. While juggling two careers in that hard, glittering city, he suffered debt, marital problems, and often, amid the gastronomic plenty, sheer hunger.

Initially Pagnol saw himself as a social satirist. Early plays produced in this vein, *Les Marchands de la Gloire* (the downside of military heroism), written with his friend Paul Nivoix, and *Jazz* (lost youth), written alone, enabled him to give up schoolteaching. In 1928 *Topaze* (corruption), with a schoolmaster as its central character, was his first big hit.

Pagnol was beginning to draw on what he knew about, and he saw that it paid off.

His marriage, meanwhile, was distinctly rocky. To relieve the boredom of a workaholic's wife, Simonne had taken a job. Marcel wanted a child; she didn't. He began an affair with the actress Orane Demazis, female lead in *Jazz*. He separated from Simonne but Orane, brought up in the conventional atmosphere of French colonial Algeria, would not live with him until he got a divorce. Simonne refused it on religious grounds.

Pagnol, in those exciting but fraught years in Paris, often pined for Marseilles. His Paris *quartier* near the Porte de St-Cloud reminded him of La Plaine: same villagey ambience; market, bistrot on the corner; knowing the waiters by their first names; being greeted with a 'Bonjour, M'sieur Pagnol' by a flowerseller. But there was not the sun, the *aïoli*, the easy laughter, and no one said *biengue* instead of *bien*.

He remembered songs from the old Alcazar Music Hall on the Cours Belsunce, with its easy-going atmosphere of a café-concert, Marseillais drinking and laughing at little tables. The revues were topical, the gags local, sending up regular butts for humour like the fishwife, the *boules*-player, the village idiot (*fada*), the Parisian who got red in the sun. They were known as 'garlic and olive oil' shows. Many French stars from Provence – Fernandel, Gilbert Bécaud, Yves Montand – made early appearances at the Alcazar. And Marcel Pagnol began to wonder if his own voice might not gain from a more earthy, popular Marseilles than the bourgeois, academic milieu he had been brought up in.

He returned to the city to observe life on the Old Port, the living Césars and Panisses. The café-owner wore a cap on the back of his head, the waterfront merchant a panama. But at *boules* or cards there was no social distinction; they played together. Of whatever class, a Marseillais can make a meal out of nothing, and nothing of disaster. A joke records how a priest is preaching that the end of the world is nigh, God will punish the impious city for its sins, tomorrow Marseilles will breathe its last gasp. A voice from the back of the church pipes up: 'I couldn't care less – I'm from Endoume.'

The caustic, ironic wit of the Marseillais, with its exaggerations and egotism, appealed to Marcel Pagnol. Witness César, belittling his son Marius's talents as an assistant ship's cook: 'They must eat well on that boat! After a month there'll be nothing but skeletons on board. It'll be a ghost ship' (*Fanny*).

Working holidays at La Treille on other plays encouraged Pagnol to explore his theme in situ. The story was pure Barber of Seville, taking place on the Rive-Neuve, the south quay of the Old Port: a girl who sells shellfish from a stall (Fanny) is in love with a café waiter (Marius) but marries a wealthy old master sailmaker (Panisse). The character of Marius was based on Louis Brouquier, a Marseilles poet who wrote for *Fortunio* and 'bent our ears with tales of the sea, his islands and boats'.

In fact, the *Fortunio* group don't seem to have had the *nostalgie de la boue* of their Paris counterparts, the post-Baudelaire poets who loved the low-life in popular bars, brothels, and dance halls. Even Pagnol himself had not realized how much he loved Marseilles till he left it. In his youth, the attraction of the Port of the Orient had eluded him. Its quaysides were just plain dirty and noisy, its back streets a warren of evil-smelling, Neapolitan laundries with washing draped above the heads of tattooed sailors and tawdry *putes*. Seedy waterfront bars, which kept out heat and flies with bead curtains and undesirables with a strong arm, were no place to enjoy an *anisette* or a *Picon-citron*. The dialogue of card-players beneath the awnings had fallen on deaf ears. 'If you can't cheat with your friends, it's not worth playing cards!' César says.

The Old Port was a dubious old acquaintance. Gradually, it became a close friend whose charm and vitality Pagnol had underrated. It is a Marseilles legend which has inspired writers, film-makers, and artists all over the world. And, as such, has come in for at least as much clichéd representation as ooh-la-la Montmartre.

Picturesque and exotic, it was Pépé le Moko's second home, a gangster's paradise across the water from Algiers. 'Come to the casbah!' murmured countless surrogate Charles Boyers. Drugs, contraband cigarettes and white slaves were as much the daily traffic as Indian cotton, Senegalese peanuts, and rice from Madagascar. And the apparently innocent violin-players on their way to the Opéra invariably packed a gat in their cases.

A *voyou* in co-respondent's shoes and snappy white cap would jump from his black Citroën and settle his accounts with the *mec* who had shipped his rosebud-lipped girl off to a brothel in Buenos Aires. After pumping him full of lead from his Browning on a steaming quayside or some deserted, blistering white rock, he would go and join the Foreign Legion. It was conveniently based in Aubagne.

Every so often the criminal legend is kept going by films like *Borsalino* and *The French Connection*; or by crimes concerning corrupt politicians, money-laundering, and Mafiosi activities associated with the Midi. Everyone loves a Marseilles scandal.

It was this cliché image, arising in the early twenties, which Marcel Pagnol tried to avoid – together with hackneyed customs and misrepresentations. It was no easy task. Even Pagnol himself falls into the trap, when Marius comments: 'I've noticed it for a long time. In Marseilles, there's nothing as painful as work.'

But the clichés are normally nicely nailed. When Marius is suspected of criminal activities and having served a prison sentence in Toulon (a rough town in those days), it is false. His 'crime' was, as a sailor, bumping into a superior officer, his 'prison' fifteen days' detention.

César, owner of the Bar de la Marine, puts a Lyonnais customer straight: 'In fact, Monsieur Brun, in Marseilles we never say *bagasse*, we never have two-pointed beards, we don't often eat *aïoli*, we leave pith-helmets to explorers. . .' *Bagasse* was anachronistic argot for *putain* (tart); in fact it has nothing to do with prostitution and was no more offensive than, say, 'Luv'. Foreign sailors from La Joliette, the huge cargo and passenger port, headed for the anonymity of bordellos in Le Panier, which was a world apart. The much smaller Vieux Port was for fishing boats, schooners, yachts and motor boats, as it is today. Its atmosphere was intimate and local, a neighbourhood where everyone knew everyone else's business and a family drama would be round the bars in two seconds.

With his astute eye and ear for spirit of place, Pagnol milked the Old Port's landmarks for every drop of atmosphere they could provide. The transporter bridge, built in 1905 and destroyed by German bombs, is naturally much better than the *tourifèle*. Paris's weedy monument may be five times higher but it's only half as wide. And, as César points out, it's the width that counts. Crossing the Old Port by the transporter bridge, Fanny gets vertiginous when she looks down. She and her mother, coming from home in Le Panier to their shellfish stall outside the Bar de la Marine, prefer to take the ferry.

Le fériboite is an indestructible emblem of Marseilles folklore, chugging backwards and forwards between the Hôtel de Ville and the Quai de Rive-Neuve. Pagnol's Escartefigue (also the name of a Toulon mayor), the ferryboat's captain, gets seasick even in the Old Port. He hates the sea, and can't think why Marius should want to be a sailor. He's delighted for the French flag to fly over distant peoples. 'But go there? IN A BOAT? Thanks a lot. I'm quite happy here.'

When César, during a card game, suggests Escartefigue is a cuckold, the patriotic captain is furious. 'Whether I'm a cuckold or not has not the slightest importance. Go on, you can insult

me, drag my name in the dirt, I couldn't care less. But I FORBID you to insult the French Navy!'

Scene of insults, reconciliations, tears, laughter, one speedily following the other, the Bar de la Marine is where the entire action of Pagnol's play takes place. César lives, breathes, eats, drinks, plays cards, and sleeps there. 'I never leave my bar. I shall die making a *Picon-citron*, and if it's allowed, I'll have myself buried under the counter.'

Pagnol's attention to domestic detail is Chekhovian in its meticulousness. Although not a great drinker himself when young, he has César expertly chill his little white wine 'so that you'd think it came from a vineyard of the North Pole'. The white wine of Cassis is reckoned to be particularly calming, and will do Panisse good after his heart attack.

Marius, however, is not much of a barman, his mind always on his projected travels. César shows him how to make a Mandarin-Citron-Curaçao correctly.

The Bar de la Marine, César's waterfront bar where most of the action takes place in Marius, *directed by Alexander Korda, with script by Marcel Pagnol, the first of the films in* The Marseilles Trilogy *(1931).*

César: First, put in a third of Curaçao. Careful, just a little third. Good. Now, a third of Citron. A little bigger. Good. Then, a BIG third of Picon.

Look at the colour. Look how pretty it is. And
finally, a LARGE third of water. That's it.

Marius: That makes four thirds. There are only three
thirds in a glass.

César: Fool! It depends on the size of the thirds!

Marius: Not at all. Even in a watering-can, there are
only three thirds.

César: (*triumphant*) So how did I put four in this
glass?

And so the argument goes on, with the *reductio ad absurdum*
of Old Port disputes.

*The ferry that was
made famous by* The
Marseilles Trilogy,
*chugging perennially
between the Town Hall
and Le Quai Rive-Neuve,
where the Bar de la
Marine is also still in
business.*

Outside the bar, working in conjunction with it, is Fanny and
Honorine's shellfish stall. César's customers like M. Brun can
order a *panaché*, a mixed platter of the day's best catch. Fanny
brings him mussels, *clovisses*, and *violets*. Local, untranslatable
shellfish lie beside prawns, shrimps, clams and oysters.

The story is simple; its convincing directness comes from the
heart. The bitter-sweet romance and family conflict stem from
the egotism of a widow and two widowers, and the dilemma of
the hero, torn between his love for the heroine and his love for
the sea.

Fanny: Love isn't everything. There are things stronger than it. . .

Marius: Yes, money. . .

Fanny: Money, the sea. . .

Marius: Each of us is heading towards the thing we love. You'll marry Panisse's money, and I'm free, I'll marry the sea. Yes, that's best for both of us.

Fanny courageously covers up Marius's departure on *La Malaisie*, so that his father César won't try to stop him and, as the schooner sails, faints in his arms.

The cliffhanger ending of *Marius* left the enchanted Parisian audience cheering for more, and over the next eight years Pagnol continued his *Marseilles Trilogy* with *Fanny* and *César*. He was lucky enough to be able to retain many of the same actors, for he owed much of the success of the play to superb casting. The Marseilles accents and mannerisms were, by and large, genuine. He took the hazardous plunge of casting a girlfriend as Fanny; Orane Demazis was no beauty but had gutsy sincerity and a determined, no-nonsense walk. Her roots in Oran, Algeria, gave her Mediterranean authenticity.

Alida Rouffe (Honorine) had been a singer at the Alcazar Music Hall. Fernand Charpin, an elegantly pleased-with-himself Panisse, was genuine Marseillais, as were Maupi (the cheeky ferryboat driver) and Delmont (the doctor). And the handsome Pierre Fresnay (Marius), though rather a matinée idol, had done his military service in Marseilles and had the right sharp tang of the sea in his accent.

But the most talked about performance was Raimu's as César. Raimu, son of a Toulon carpet-maker, was said to be dumb, difficult, and a director's albatross. But he had the intelligence to see that the role of César, to whom nothing much happens, was better than that of Panisse, who was pivotal. César was the archetypal Mediterranean father, firmly believing himself to be in control, whatever might occur to the contrary, and would preside over the trilogy like a waterfront godfather. Raimu didn't play César, he *was* César. Always wearing his cap indoors, constantly adjusting it according to mood, catching it naturally when it fell off during an argument; wiping the sweat off his neck; wrestling with the brim of a panama hat which refuses to turn down; pushing the jigger of bottles right into the glass; building his rages to apoplectic delirium; imitating terrible illnesses; exaggerating, cajoling, yelling, mocking; surprising with his softness of heart behind the tyrant's front.

The actors, particularly the genuine Marseillais, felt Pagnol had written with typical Marseilles exaggeration and that their roles bordered on caricatures. Perhaps. But the Parisian audience, used to plays with Provençal characters as phoney as Mummersetshire servants in English drawing-room comedy, were thankful for a breath of real 'garlic and olive oil'.

Marcel Pagnol was now driving a Hispano-Suiza. He was published by Fasquelle, in company with Zola, Maeterlinck, and Rostand. He was invited to stay with his impresarios, the Volterras, at a simple little Provençal fishing village (as it was then) called St-Tropez. He met artists and writers like Matisse and Bonnard; Colette at her house, La Treille Muscate; Mistinguett, dancing under the plane trees; and the film director René Clair.

Rich and famous and very handsome, Marcel Pagnol was a *tombeur des filles*. He could have had society women and world famous actresses, but they bored him. He had not changed his bohemian lifestyle. Since his separation from his wife, Simonne, things had become tense with his leading lady, Orane. And a Tiller girl from the Casino revue, Kitty Murphy, took his fancy. Kitty was eighteen, the same age as Fanny.

Pagnol had brought the curtain down on Fanny fainting for a reason which was to become clear in the next instalment of the trilogy. She was pregnant. And as life mirrored art, so Kitty became pregnant by Marcel. He had wanted a child badly. Simonne's refusal was now made up for by the birth of a son, Jacques, in 1930. As Marcel was not yet divorced the child kept his mother's name. He was a joy to both parents, and Kitty seemed content with the healthy, country life Marcel made for them in deepest France.

The bourgeois morality of his own parents, Joseph and Augustine, was now well and truly over for Marcel. He was a free spirit, living his own adventure. He knew what he was writing about.

To some extent meridionally macho, in other ways ahead of his time, Pagnol championed women's independence of spirit. So Fanny announces: 'My idea, if Maman allows it, would be not to get married, and bring up the child by working, while I wait for his father to return. If he returns' (*Fanny*).

Marcel Pagnol returned many times to Marseilles. 'To reach the universal, stay at home' had never been more true. And from *Marius* onwards, his most important work was associated with Provence, much of it for the cinema.

The Marseilles Trilogy had to continue; audiences were eager to know whether Marius and Fanny would get together again.

Marius turned out not to be quite the globe-trotter his name suggested. He may have had a world-conquering Roman general's name but, as he wrote in a letter to his father, he did not get around to visiting 'the famous Greek city of Athens, which was once a Roman fortress'. And he had not really inherited the maritime daring of his Phocian ancestors, as they set forth from Lacydon to explore an unknown world. Marius

Fanny (Orane Demazis) has fainted after her lover Marius (Pierre Fresnay) sails from Marseilles Old Port, causing commotion at the Bar de la Marine (Fanny, 1932).

had more in common with the other landlubbers of the twentieth-century Old Port, including his author, thankful to have their feet on terra firma. As César puts it: 'Poor wretch! What's it all for, this madness wanting to float on water, eat tinned food, sleep hanging from the ceiling, not to be able to pour a glass without spilling it, impossible to play *pétanque* or billiards, and all that in the midst of tempests, cyclones, and sharks!' (*Marius*).

When Marius returns, however, Fanny is married to Panisse who has adopted her son, Césariot, and brought him up as his own. Marius tries to claim the child and reinstate himself with Fanny, but César prevents him from breaking up a reasonably happy home. Once again Marius leaves Marseilles, this time as a son banished by his father.

The heightened, meridional emotions and mordant wit of *The Marseilles Trilogy* made perfect popular cinema. And in 1930 Marcel Pagnol began to turn away from the theatre towards the new art form of the talking picture. A trip to the London Palladium, then a picture house, to see *Broadway Melody*, sparked off a passion that was to last him a lifetime. Cinema, in his view, had these advantages over theatre: dialogue was more natural, less declamatory; wherever they were sitting, an audience heard the same whisper or cry and had the same view; characters could be presented in realistic, familiar surroundings – César in his bar, Panisse in his emporium, Fanny at her fish stall, Marius in his garage, with mere cuts for a change of scene; and the finished movie, if it was a contemporary subject, recorded that precise moment of history in fashion, décor, and speech.

These, and many other theories, led Pagnol to be unpopular both with theatre people for what they saw as desertion, and with cinema people for thinking he knew it all. He was both deserter and Johnny-come-lately.

At the studios, it was different. Technicians admired his audacity – he could, after all, have rested on his theatre laurels – and taught him everything they could about sound, lighting, laboratory development and printing of film. His fame was already international. Hollywood studios were after the rights of his plays. Paramount's man in Paris, the hard-drinking Bob Kane, invited him out to lunch, believing him to be a manufacturer of arc lamps. Somewhat offended, the celebrated author said his name was Marcel Pagnol and he did not make arc lamps. 'So what do you do, Mister Pagnol?'

Bob Kane was not nearly as crass as he sounded. He and Pagnol became good friends. He set up the film of *Marius* –

with German and Swedish versions to be shot with different
casts on the same set, all to be directed by Alexander Korda.
Although he acceded to many of Pagnol's tough business
demands, he insisted that the French version should have a
director with a track record. Pagnol would write the script;
Korda would direct.

Pagnol felt that a Hollywood Hungarian might be a little out
of place in the Old Port and not sufficiently *au fait* with what
was basically a 'garlic and olive oil' show. He was, therefore,
pleasantly surprised to find that the young, cigar-smoking
Korda, within forty-eight hours of arriving in France, had seen
the stage play twice, and would go for a third time that evening.
'We will take all your actors,' he added.

Raimiou, as Bob Kane called the star, could not be properly
recorded, according to the soundman from Western Electric. His
voice was not 'phonogenic'. As it was one of the most
characterful voices on the French stage and had sung on a
hundred gramophone records, how was this possible? Korda
warned the soundman that Raimu was irreplaceable, but *he* was
not. He had better get it right.

Raimu yelled his lines into the mike: 'Monsieur Brun, don't
tell anyone Escartefigue is a cuckold! It could get around!' The
soundman winced and begged him to lose a few decibels; he
had nearly punctured an eardrum. Raimu duly lowered his
voice and murmured: 'Your American machines don't
understand French. Now, as it's midday, come and have an
apéritif with me and, to get your ear used to my trombone, I
shall recount you a fable or two.' From then on, Raimu's voice
was perfectly recorded.

So was Marseilles by the lighting cameraman. *Marius* (1931)
was one of the earliest French talkies to show even a minimum
of real locations. With each film of the trilogy, techniques
improved and more and more locations were used, with
backgrounds of a great maritime city's vitality and movement,
landmarks which, in the play, could only be referred to. Behind
the main credits of *Marius*, sailboats and a schooner establish
the Old Port, with the transporter bridge; then follows a
panning shot of the sea, the port and the city from the heights
of Notre-Dame-de-la-Garde.

Taking their siestas, Panisse lies asleep on a bench, César on
a banquette in his bar. Marius, one cigarette behind his ear,
another in the corner of his mouth, sprinkles the terrace with
water to cool it down, and gazes longingly at *La Malaisie*, the
four-master in the harbour. So much is set up so economically –
the sea, the city, the sizzling heat, and Marius, the dreaming waiter.

Visual details later underpin character: Honorine hanging up her fish-scales; Marius's room with model sailboats in bottles, African masks on the wall; César breakfasting on a glass of red wine and a dish of olives, or cooking a lonely widower's dinner. Marius and Fanny's night of love is followed by a lyrical shot of the port at dawn, the lighthouse, and waves breaking on rocks – not then the clichéd symbol for love-making it became. And the romantic end is reinforced, after Fanny's faint, by the majestic sight of *La Malaisie* heading out past the lighthouse, carrying Marius towards his destiny.

Fanny (1932) is the most accomplished of the three films. The stage play featured even more Old Port locations than *Marius*. An added factor was the confidence, after the smash of *Marius*, of the largely unchanged cast and crew; they were like a local team, many of its members coming from Marseilles, Toulon, Arles, Aix and Nice, happy to be playing together again. Pagnol's sets became famous for their team spirit; making movies was a kind of sport to him.

The director, Marc Allégret, was the only outsider; Pagnol was afraid he would be too sophisticatedly Parisian. As the team's producer-writer 'captain', Pagnol encouraged Allégret to risk more and more elaborate exterior shooting, like the long, brilliant tracking shot, with the camera mounted on a truck, following Fanny (Orane Demazis) walking among trams, cars and people on a busy Vieux Port quayside.

The slanging matches of Pagnol and Allégret were all in a Marseilles day's work. There were problems of the heart, too. Kitty Murphy did not like the sun, so she did not join Marcel on location. Inevitably, working happily with Orane, he found himself in bed with her again, and she was later to bear his son, Jean-Pierre.

Life continued to mirror art. Marseilles composer, Vincent Scotto, wrote just the right poignant waltz theme to accompany Fanny on her climb to Notre-Dame-de-la-Garde to ask forgiveness from the Virgin for bearing Marius's child. The vast city spreads out behind her, emphasizing her isolation.

Opposite: Fanny's mother, Honorine (Alida Rouffe, second from left), working at her shop in the Old Port fish market. The film Fanny *was directed by Marc Allégret, with a script by Marcel Pagnol based on his hit play (1932).*

There are other memorable location images: César stopping the tram while he measures his *boule*'s position; Panisse, all dressed up to propose to Fanny, having his hat knocked off by the cheeky boatman (Maupi), who pretends he thought Panisse was an American ('Next time you see an American, it better not be me!'); Fanny and Panisse's wedding procession, the party crossing the Old Port by *le fériboîte*; Honorine and César proudly looking after their baby grandson in the Pharo park, high above the Old Port.

The third instalment of *The Marseilles Trilogy*, *César*, first appeared as a film, not a play. The action takes place twenty years after the marriage of Fanny and Panisse. Panisse dies. Césariot finds out he is Marius's son, not Panisse's, and is furious with Fanny. Secretly, he finds his real father and, after a change of heart encouraged by César, brings Marius and Fanny together again.

Pagnol himself directed *César*, opening up the story still further to give his audience fresh images of the Provençal coast. Although the film becomes bogged down in its complicated though brilliantly crafted plot concerning Marius's suspected crimes, Pagnol relishes taking us to Toulon, where the exiled Marius owns a garage. Toulon, at the time, had an even worse reputation for crime, prostitution and drugs than Marseilles. If Marius was to be suspect, Pagnol would give Toulon the bad image rather than the city of his youth.

Action also takes place in the fishing villages and creeks where Panisse went on Sunday outings, or where César took Marius as a child: a villa at Cassis; fishing at Cap Couronne; the enchanting village of Niolon, still unspoilt today; and Carry-le-Rouet, a seaside town which rates a Michelin two-star fish restaurant.

Stars even harder to obtain caused a delay in shooting *César* until 1936. Charpin, Fresnay and Raimu were by now in great demand, but Pagnol wisely hung out till they were free. Raimu had become even more difficult. He hated location shooting, autograph hunters, the mistral, and being given directions by 'young' Marcel Pagnol (aged forty-one) in public. Nor could he learn the last-minute changes of dialogue Pagnol loved to throw at his actors. Raimu was now a studio-orientated actor, used to the kow-towing of starstruck hack directors. Pagnol put up with the insults, and gave as good as he got. This ability to externalize resentment in shouting matches is a typically southern trait. In cold climates, grudges are a source of inner warmth and borne in cosy silence.

However, it was not just on the set and in Pagnol's scripts that these heightened emotions let rip. Certain Marseillais expressed hurt feelings about the way Pagnol had portrayed them. A prudish respectability made them flinch at seeing themselves as Pagnol saw them: mercurial, venal, egotistical, manipulative, sentimental. Pagnol's local detractors in the prissier parts of town turned blind eyes and deaf ears to the generosity, wit, compassion, and the Provençal support system depicted throughout *The Marseilles Trilogy*. The characters care about each other, so we care about them.

Opposite: Pagnolian figures in a window, Cours d'Estienne d'Orves, Marseilles.

César: (*calmly*) Marius, you're a liar.

Marius: Why?

César: (*violently*) Because you're lying. Liar! You love Fanny. Aren't you mad with rage because someone else wants to take her and you're refusing to marry her? You've become intolerable! If you're crazy, tell me frankly – and I'll send you to the madhouse and we'll say no more about it (*Marius*).

Honorine rages against men when she hears that Fanny is pregnant by Marius, yelling at her sister that he must be the culprit because she hasn't slept with the whole of Marseilles: 'Oh! I'll have him in court, I will! Into prison with him, bashing stones! . . Holy Mother, let the devils of the sea eat the boat from under him! May the winkles pick him to bits, the man who ruined the life of my poor little innocent girl!' (*Fanny*).

Nearly always, melodrama is tempered by a humorous turn of phrase, sentimentality by a toughness of spirit. César can get in a rage about very little but resists expressing his deeper feelings for Marius, so that when he does find the words it is all the more moving: 'You know, sometimes I tell you you poison my existence, but it's not true' (*Marius*).

Panisse, too, has the same basic generosity of spirit, whatever insults he may receive from César. He may not care about Marius's claim to Fanny, but he respects his wife's wishes: 'Fanny, if you want a separation, I will take all the blame for it.' What he will not do, however, is to give up 'his' child, his heir. Pagnol's characters are never entirely altruistic; their pride makes them human.

But the more prudish Marseillais chose only to see the flaws. 'We're never like that,' they said. Nor did they appreciate the Provençal *argot* of the dialogue, with its heady sprinkling of words like *jobastre* (fall guy), *fada* (loony), *peuchère* (poor chap), *coquin de sort* (lousy luck); nor the often bawdy insults, as from Panisse to Escartefigue: 'A boat which has a propeller at each end is a boat which is always going backwards. There's no forwards on this boat. It has two arseholes, plus you, that makes three!' (*Marius*). Nor were the detractors won over by the authenticity of the food and drink: *anisette, mousseaux,* pastis (drunk less in those days than now), *Picon-citron*, fish soup, snails, Aubagne sausage, dried cod, beef stew with olives, and red mullet.

There were secret places to find the best fish. Marius has inherited a fisherman's notebook, with precise instructions: 'Off the lighthouse, level with the signal station, just opposite the belltower of St-Vincent. Depth sixteen metres . . . Best in summer on a calm day' (*César*). That was off Toulon harbour. A contemporary inheritor of the notebook would no doubt have to go farther afield – off the unpolluted *calanques* (fiord-like creeks) which indent the barren, mountainous coastline between Cap Croisette and Cassis.

Hard to believe as it is, Pagnol himself was as much a land-lubber as his Old Port characters. He mistrusted the sea, hardly ever swam in it, and never owned a yacht. Inevitably, he began to look inland for new inspiration – to the wilder uplands.

PAGNOL'S PROVENCE

The **Old Port** and its few remaining Pagnolian sights are best seen on foot. A good place to start is **Le Parc du Pharo** with a view from the mouth of the harbour much as the Phocians and Marius returning from the South Seas must have seen it. The park's palace was built by Napoleon III for Empress Eugénie but they never lived in it.

Just before the **Quai de Rive-Neuve** which runs along the south side of the port, on your left is the **Quai Marcel-Pagnol** nestling beneath the **St-Nicholas Fort.** Ships' chandlers, modern versions of Panisse's sailmaking business, serve the yacht marina. The **Bar de la Marine**, with its pretty waitresses and chic parasols, bears little resemblance to César's bar apart from the same logo, but it has a collection of Pagnol memora-bilia inside. It is pleasant to people-watch over a pastis, but you're more likely to see Pagnolian card-players in the few remaining hole-in-the-wall joints along the waterfront. Panisse's emporium is an Alsatian brasserie.

Today's Old Port blatantly caters for tourists, and does it elegantly. The pedestrian area of the **Cours d'Estienne d'Orves**, once the Arsenal and later boasting the mansions of rich merchants, and the beautiful **Carré Thiars** and **Rue St-Saens** are where the action is. Restaurants, jazz clubs, and discos are open till all hours. If you want to buy Pagnol books, an unusual bookstore is Les Arcenaulx (also a restaurant and coffee shop) on the Cours. The Old Port is constantly surprising. Within twenty-four hours I witnessed the Veterans Celebration of the Fiftieth Anniversary of the Allied Landings in southern France at the **Hôtel de Ville** – all military pomp, brass bands, and servicemen young and old; and a French Antilles Carnival parading on the **Quai des Belges** with steel bands, floats, combining Caribbean with Marseillais exuberance.

Overleaf: A sailing ship in Marseilles' Old Port, reminiscent of La Malaisie, *on which* Marius *goes to sea in* Marius *and returns in* Fanny.

The Quai des Belges is where the main street, **La Canebière**, meets the port. At apéritif time, well-heeled Marseillais meet at the least touristy of the waterfront cafés, the New York Brasserie. Across the street on the quayside, in the early morning, modern Fannys and Honorines set up their stalls at the fish market.

Film buffs should not miss the nearby **Musée Provençal du Cinéma** (3 Rue Colbert), a film centre which pays homage to the many Marseillais cinéastes besides Pagnol.

A walk up steep steps behind the town hall on the **Quai du Port** takes you to where Fanny and Honorine lived. The narrow streets festooned with laundry of **Le Panier** quarter (now respectable) are genuinely Pagnolian. Not to be missed is **La Vieille Charité**, a multi-media cultural centre in a seventeenth-century hospice, its chapel beautifully converted into an art gallery.

End the walk by taking the **ferry** back across the harbour. A young Escartefigue moves to the other side of the wheel for the return trip, a Ricard bottle perched on top of the control panel. It must be only for show, because the two-minute crossing is most soberly manoeuvred.

Good hotels round the Old Port are Sofitel (expensive) near the lighthouse; the Pullman Buveau (expensive to moderate), where Georges Sand and Chopin once stayed; and the Hermès (inexpensive), where the penthouse is a bargain with its after-dark view across the harbour lights to the expertly floodlit **Notre-Dame-de-la-Garde**, which seems to float in mid-air.

A gem of a hotel is the beautifully furnished Le Petit Nice (expensive), overlooking the sea on the Corniche. It has a two-star Michelin restaurant serving Provençal-inspired delicacies fresh from the market and sea.

Bouillabaisse is chancy. Avoid restaurants on the Quai du Port – except Le Miramar, which is well up to the standards of Pagnol's day. Secret recipes, like fishermen's secret notebooks, abound: everyone's is 'the best', of course. The nineteenth-century Provençal cookbook, *Reboul*, lists some forty usable fish. But as it was originally a fisherman's soup, made from fish just caught and boiled on the beach, it still depends on the catch of the day. Four different types of fish – from a choice of, among others, *rascasse*, red mullet, burbot, John Dory, conger eel, red gurnard – are marinaded overnight in tomatoes, onions, peppers, garlic, olive oil, saffron, and fennel. *Bouillabaisse* makes a two-course meal – a fish soup, followed by the fish with pungent, saffron-yellow potatoes. The addition of lobster is not authentic – for rich tourists only.

Be warned: good local fish dishes are expensive. The best *bouillabaisses* (or some of 'the best'), *bourrides* and *panachés* (mixed plateaux of seafood) are to be found at Le Miramar in the Old Port, Chez Paul in Rue St-Saens, Calypso on the Corniche, L'Epuisette and Chez Fonfon in the lively fishing harbour of the Vallon des Auffes and, my own particular favourite, Chez Aldo at Montredon: I like the easy-going ambience, off-beat seaside locale, and Max, the chef, insists on reservations for *bouillabaisse* the day before so that he can correctly marinade the fish overnight. Max, in the Pagnol manner, is a perfectionist.

For places to eat in both Niolon and Carry, see Chapter VI (page 138).

CHAPTER FIVE

THE BAKER'S WIFE

The Bread of Life – Provençal country breads, without which the villagers in La Femme du Boulanger *cannot survive.*

At the age of thirty-seven, Marcel Pagnol was awarded the Légion d'Honneur. In the same batch of recipients was another important young Provençal writer, the novelist Jean Giono.

A further coincidence was to unite the two writers in a volatile and highly productive partnership. After the première of *Marius* in Brussels, Pagnol happened to buy a magazine at the railway station before catching the train back to Paris. He was astonished to read an extract from Jean Giono's novel *Jean le Bleu*, entitled 'La Femme du Boulanger'. He himself had just completed a story in similar vein, entitled *Le Boulanger Amable*.

Some writers would have gone straight to the Wagon-Restaurant and ordered a triple cognac. Not Pagnol; he was far too astute. He had always admired Giono's evocation of rural life on the Plateau de Vaucluse, and in the Basses-Alpes and Haute-Provence – the uplands of Provence which he had hardly visited except for his teaching stint at Digne. Giono pulled no punches in his descriptions of the struggle to survive in isolated farms and hilltop villages. The flight from the land since the Industrial Revolution saddened Giono, and he greatly admired the peasants who hung on to what he saw as the 'real riches', rejecting the soulless employment in city industry.

Born in the market town of Manosque in 1895, Giono was only a month older than Pagnol. Giono's was a world of sombre wintry fields, farmhouses blasted by the mistral, gruelling harvests beneath a relentless sun, dusty poplar-lined roads, ponds loud with the croak of frogs. Giono had no illusions. 'Whoever loves Provence, loves the world', he wrote. He created universal, mythic stories based on a very real, contemporary plight. His peasants seemed trapped in an obsolescent way of life. They could free themselves, though: in refusing to conform to the mechanization of modern society, through their own labour and love of the land, they would rediscover the earth's natural rhythms.

A Hellenistic pantheism, Giono believed, was preferable to Christianity – a belief in the gods of the earth to bring salvation in this world rather than the village Curé's happiness in the next. The days were round, like nature's year, a cycle of births and deaths. The sun died and was reborn; the leaves died and were reborn. Inevitably the spring came again and, in its burgeoning warmth, a peasant grew strong with his crop – unless a bad harvest or a forest fire made him the victim of destiny. The olive, which was sometimes killed by frost, was the tree of Minerva/Athena, goddess of wisdom and intelligence. It was the tree of peace too; Giono wrote: 'Fuck war, long live life and long live anarchy!'

His romantic anti-militarism was shared by Pagnol. They shared other things, too: foreign antecedents – Pagnol Spanish, Giono Italian; an enthusiasm for Shakespeare and Virgil; a natural affinity with shepherds, goatherds, plants and animals; a mistrust of folklore and a dedication to authenticity.

Pagnol realized they could not both use a story about a baker who could no longer bake the village bread. And, on that Brussels–Paris express, he generously conceded that Giono had the edge.

It was not entirely impartial. Pagnol had become a part-time Parisian; Giono lived permanently in Manosque. Wisely, Pagnol realized Giono had a deeper knowledge of this beautiful but rugged interior, between the Lubéron and La Montagne de Lure, which provided such richly filmic stories. On his arrival in Paris, Pagnol set about procuring the film rights, not only of 'La Femme du Boulanger', but other Giono works. Giono, naturally, was delighted.

It came at just the right moment. *Marius* and *Fanny* were thought by movie buffs to be 'filmed plays' not 'screenplays'. As Pagnol tended to value the 'talking' more than the 'picture', there is some justification for this: his dialogue scenes were theatre-length. Now, with screen adaptations of such a highly visual novelist as Jean Giono, he could rival the Wild West with the Wild North. Even the north of Provence seemed like a million miles from the Old Port of Marseilles.

In 1933 he followed in the steps of United Artists (Douglas Fairbanks, Mary Pickford and Charlie Chaplin) and founded United Authors. One of its first productions was *Jofroi*, with Pagnol writing directly for the screen for the first time an adaptation of a ten-page Giono story, 'Jofroi de la Maussan'. He completed the script in four days.

Giono liked the way Pagnol worked as writer-director-producer. An artisanal ambience was created, and although Jofroi's lost hamlet was meant to be near Manosque in the Basses-Alpes, La Treille was the perfect location. Locals had known Pagnol since childhood and called him 'Marcel'. They found lodgings for actors and technicians. The Pagnol 'family' was back – even his brother, René, was production manager. Meals were riotous, with Pagnol one of the boys, a democratic *patron* who believed that the best results were achieved by everyone combining work with pleasure. The weather was perfect, a golden autumn.

Jofroi, a short, slight, dark comedy, needed just the lightness of touch that Pagnol, with a little help from the weather, so carefully created. He was, as usual, taking risks: a minimum of interiors, most scenes outdoors with bird song to test the temper of the soundman; and an untried actor in the title role – the composer, Vincent Scotto.

Scotto was at the height of his fame. He had written hits for Josephine Baker like 'J'ai Deux Amours' and the waltz theme of *Fanny*. When Pagnol first read the script to his team, he asked Scotto who he thought could play Jofroi. 'Me,' said the composer without hesitation. Pagnol thought he was joking; he had an eccentric sense of humour, maintaining that gravity was not caused by the earth's pull but by the universe's repulsion. Nothing would put him off; the small, beak-nosed composer with jet-black hair and a big moustache greyed up a little, put on a peasant's corduroy suit and auditioned a scene which touched Pagnol with its naturalness. Scotto had not been joking.

The second role, Fonse, was played by another non-actor who was to join the 'family', Henri Poupon. A Provençal natural like Scotto, Poupon was a lyric writer who entertained people on the set with his songs. He was also a champion *boules* player, and turned down a role which could have made him as big a star as Raimu, simply because it interfered with an important match. His debts were legendary; he gave banquets but dressed like a beggar. A Bandol hotelier allowed him to stay cheap in his hotel as long as Poupon agreed to move rooms during the summer season; gradually he was demoted from a first-floor suite via a second-floor bedroom without bath to a top-floor garret. In September he started the move back down to luxury.

Another who was to become a Pagnol 'family' member was Charles Blavette, who plays Fonse's friend, Tonin. He had a profitable canned food factory, but had always wanted to act. Again Pagnol was surprised by his naturalness and the way he spoke his Provençal dialogue. He became a charming supporting actor whose face people were always glad to see – and often did in Pagnol films.

Jofroi begins in a Manosque notary's office. An establishing shot of the town is dispensed with, and we see the notary reading the act of sale between Jofroi and Fonse for a small orchard at Jofroi's farm, La Maussan. Jofroi's wife Barbe, dressed in black, sits meekly in the corner, although the orchard, like the rest of the farm, is communal property between husband and wife.

Jofroi is described, at different moments of the scene as

'severe, greedy, angry, furious'. Barbe, on the other hand, is 'timid, humble, modest, gentle'. But it's Barbe who first suggests they see the colour of Fonse's money, appealing to the notary when the two peasants get into a quarrel. The bickering gets even more heated when the notary insists on Barbe signing the document. That's the law. Jofroi claims the orchard is his, not Barbe's. Then the old man suddenly relents when Barbe says it will be an honour for her to sign the papers with him – like they did at their marriage. Jofroi tenderly takes her hand and leads her from her corner to the notary's table.

The story goes on to tell how a terrible feud develops between Jofroi and Fonse. Jofroi does not want a single tree of the orchard he has sold to be cut down; Fonse sees it as his inalienable right as the orchard's purchaser. Jofroi threatens suicide to save his trees and the dark comedy revolves around his various attempts. Saved from mortal sin, Jofroi dies a natural death from apoplexy. Out of respect, Fonse will save a few trees in his memory. Trees are shade. Trees are peace.

Pagnol hits the right rural note: Fonse slowly helping his mule pull a cart up a hill between stony, terraced fields – with 'yellow grass and thyme surrounding several olive trees' (Pagnol puts colours in his scripts, even for black-and-white photography!); a peasant taking a nap under a tree; Fonse determined to sow his wheat before the new moon; the old hags of the village cursing Fonse with witchlike cries of 'Alibifistoc!' for causing Jofroi's suicide attempts; the village *fête*, with villagers huddled in overcoats against an early cold snap, dancing an energetic *pasa doble* to keep warm.

Jean Giono could not come to terms with the cinematic elaboration of his short story. He didn't criticize Pagnol personally but the cinema in general, which, he reckoned, took over and savagely transformed his tale. It made mischief, too. He describes taking two friends to the film in Manosque: they had been involved in the rural squabble on which Giono had based his original story. One friend was Giono's 'Fonse'; the other the widow of Giono's 'Jofroi'. The two families had been reconciled for years, but that visit to the cinema opened up old wounds. They didn't speak for months. And Giono had only himself to blame for taking them on such a tactless cinema outing.

Considered to be the first film in the neo-realist style, later to be adopted by Italian cinéastes, *Jofroi* was not shown in the United States until 1956, when it won the critics' award for Best Foreign Film. One critic wrote of Vincent Scotto: 'It is surprising that this admirable performer is still unknown in America.

He is the only living actor comparable to Charlie Chaplin.'

Another great Provençal actor was now to come into Marcel Pagnol's life: Fernandel. He was cast as the farmhand, Saturnin, in the next Giono story 'Un de Baumugnes', made as *Angèle* (1934). Its new title followed Pagnol's insistence on the classical tradition of calling a work by the name of the character whose storyline predominated, so that the audience's attention should be focused (as in *Hamlet, Medea, Le Cid* and *Phèdre*). Pagnol had once again taken liberties with Giono's original. The man from Baumugnes, Albin, gives precedence to the girl he loves, Angèle. And Fernandel, as the amiable, simple-minded go-between, part scapegoat and part guardian angel, brings them together and steals the show in the process.

A comic genius with a seriously insecure nature, Fernandel did not fit easily into the Pagnol 'family'. He had an inferiority complex about his lack of education; Pagnol was too much of a *prof* for his taste. Fernandel took offence easily and he hated the leisurely pace of filming, the long meals, siestas, card games, and laughter that he often took to be at his expense. He was playing in an operetta in Marseilles at the time, and was terrified of being late for a show.

One can sympathize with Fernandel. It's never easy to be the new boy at a cliquey school. And, for all his suffering he turned in a touching, confident and comic performance under Pagnol's direction.

Pagnol was glad to have two old faithfuls on the show: Orane Demazis as Angèle and Henri Poupon as her father, Clarius. Blavette also made an appearance as a knife-grinder, and Delmont (the doctor in *César*) was the itinerant farm worker, Amadée. Andrex, a flashily handsome actor known for his gangster roles, played Le Louis, the Marseilles pimp.

Again, Pagnol shot the Haute-Provence locations in the hills near Aubagne. When he became rich he had purchased fifty-seven acres of land around Les Barres de St-Esprit, where he shot exteriors for some of his most successful films in the 1930s. The word *barre*, used by Provençals, has a precise meaning – a bar of rock running along the side of a hill, often between pine woods. 'Beyond the valley a long hill stretched out. It had the shape of a warship with three decks, one set slightly back from the other. It carried three pine woods, separated by escarpments of grey rock' (*La Gloire de Mon Père*). Nowadays children compare the sloping head of Les Barres de St-Esprit with a TGV (high-speed train) engine rather than a warship.

Marius ('Mius') Brouquier, Pagnol's faithful builder, needed water to restore an abandoned farmhouse in the valley below.

From Carry-le-Rouet Pagnol brought a water-diviner cleric, Abbé Cuque, who held the rod that found the water that made the cement that filled the cracks of La Ferme Angèle that Mius built. 'It is a modest farm tucked away in a dip of a little valley. In front, an arid terrace, surrounded by low dry-stone walls. Beyond, a sparse field, bordered by a pine wood which descends from hills baked by the sun' (Angèle).

Angèle, daughter of farmer Clarius, runs away with Le Louis to Marseilles and becomes a prostitute. Farmhand Saturnin rescues her and brings her back to the farm where her dour father imprisons her and her baby in a cellar to avoid family disgrace. She is saved by the love of Albin, the decent mountain boy. He persuades Clarius to release her and forget his shame. Albin does not care about her past; he wants to marry her and take her and the baby to the mountains of Provence where 'there's grass everywhere and almond trees . . . streams of clear water'.

The film contains interesting information about Provence. For instance, the precarious life of itinerant farm workers: as Albin's friend, Amadée, puts it to Clarius, 'They don't want me on the big farms. If you don't want me on a small one, I'll be dead.'

Albin's harmonica-playing has its roots in Baumugnes's history. In the Wars of Religion, he explains, his ancestors had the tips of their tongues cut off by the enemy so that they couldn't sing their hymns any more. Kicked out of their homes, they fled to the mountains and founded Baumugnes. As they couldn't speak to each other, they invented a means of communication by harmonica. Members of future generations, who could communicate normally, kept the custom of calling children and rounding up animals by harmonica in memory of their ancestors.

Fernandel delivers a speech about country loyalties, showing Pagnol's writing at its most compassionate and earthy.

> It's as though someone said to me: 'Our Angèle's fallen in the manure.' Then I'd go and take her in my arms, and I'd give her a good wash. And I'd clean her nails with match ends, and I'd soak her hair in lavender water till there wasn't a straw, not a spot, not a speck, nothing. And I'd make her clean as water, and she'd be as beautiful as before. Because, you know, friendship cleans everything, everything, everything. . .

Overleaf: Ruins of the Ferme d'Angèle, a farmhouse in Vallon de Marcellin near La Treille which was the setting for the film Angèle.

Angèle opened in Marseilles and Fernandel stole all the notices – to the chagrin of the excellent Orane Demazis and

Henri Poupon. A star was born, and Fernandel's attitude to Pagnol changed; whatever fights they had later, he was eternally grateful to him for that first important role.

If *Jofroi* had been a gem, *Angèle* was a triumph. The more highbrow film critics poured their usual vitriol on Pagnol who was still considered to be a theatrical *parvenu* and amateur cinéaste – with a suspect commercial flair. Now, with the huge box office success of *Angèle*, his name on the bill meant as much as Raimu's. He was a star. Jean Renoir, a few weeks after the film's opening, described him as 'the greatest cinematographic author alive today'. Hit followed hit – with a slight hiccup in *Cigalon* (1935), a short comedy which unwisely laughed at French gastronomy, tantamount to blasphemy in those days. Pagnol said: 'This film makes me laugh more than anything I've done, but I'm the only one.' It soon disappeared from the screens but later, in a stage play version, proved to be a great success with amateur theatrical societies.

The village of La Treille played many roles. The esplanade was used in *Jofroi*, and the restaurant in *Cigalon*, which still exists by that name. It now serves much better food than did the perverse chef, Cigalon, who in the film serves no food at all – except to himself. We hear about food to make the mouth water: the Marseillais speciality *pieds et paquets*, steaming beef stews, *bouillabaisse*, cannelloni, spit-roast guineafowl, and a fifteen-year-old Burgundy which 'will dance on your tongue . . . caress your lips like a kiss'. But Cigalon (played by Arnaudy) resolutely refuses to cook any of it for mere bourgeois Sunday visitors – not even an omelette. When a Count appears at the restaurant, however, the snobbish Cigalon goes to work. His canned lobsters explode, while a rival restaurateur accuses him of serving sausage made of donkey. To Cigalon's chagrin, the Count turns out to be a petty crook who can't pay his bill.

Picking himself up with *César* (1936), Pagnol was at the height of his powers; as was Jean Giono. Far from coasting on his commercial success, Pagnol now tackled one of Giono's most symbolic and poetic Provençal novels, *Regain* (1937).

Following his own reservations about the added Marseilles low-life sequence in *Angèle*, Giono now exercised his right to collaborate on the script. Pagnol was delighted. It was his most ambitious film so far, and he welcomed Giono's authority on the wilds of Provence.

Giono came to Paris, but only for a few days. He and Pagnol soon discovered that, as writers, they were solo performers. Giono couldn't wait to get back to Manosque and leave the script in the capable hands of the maestro. He did visit the location, however, where he enjoyed the artisanal ambience; it was like getting in the harvest – hard work done in a spirit of comradeship.

Pagnol once again made use of his beloved hills to recreate the Plateau de Vaucluse. The ruined village of Redortiers, inspiration for Giono's original story, was in the deserted hills near Banon, a small upland town with no hotel facilities for cast and crew.

Mius Brouquier graduated from restoring a farmhouse for *Angèle* to constructing the elements of a whole village in a state of collapse on a pine-covered bluff of Les Barres de St-Esprit. It was such a convincing landmark that airline pilots were confused not to find 'Aubignane', as Redortiers was called in novel and film, on their maps. All they would spot now – with very good eyes – are the ruins of ruins: vestiges of an archway and the house of Panturle, the film's earthy hero.

Church, archway, square, fountain and baker's shop took twenty builders to construct, and dynamite was needed to level the rocky site. When a donkey lost its life humping materials up the rough path to the construction site, four-footed transport was replaced by a pulley system. The builders slept in a dormitory while crew and cast commuted from nearby Marseilles. Meals were brought by the Marseilles restaurateur Léon from his Prado restaurant. On a visit to the location, the film's composer Arthur Honegger (one of 'Les Six', the group of avant garde composers which included the Provençal, Darius Milhaud) found himself humping sacks of cement and seems to have thoroughly enjoyed himself.

Taking pity on the star, Fernandel, who had courageously taken on a less sympathetic role than he was now known for, Pagnol worked nights during shooting to lighten the part. But nights were not his best writing time. Despite his anarchic, anti-Establishment humour, the result was broad comedy, rather than savage satire. Fernandel's laboured routine with the French equivalent of the Keystone Cops was the only jarring note in the actor's otherwise convincing performance. The fact Pagnol allowed it shows that he was not really at home with this venture.

Once again playing 'destiny', Fernandel is Gédémus, the knife-grinder with a mean streak who unwittingly brings together two unlikely lovers, Panturle and Arsule. Arsule is an itinerant cabaret singer. Rescued by Gédémus from a brutal life, she finds her new one, pulling his cart up steep hills, no great improvement. She leaves Gédémus for the peasant Panturle, whose purity of spirit reforms her. Together they revive the deserted village of Aubignane.

Giono is urging a return to a respect for rural values; he was a Green ahead of his time. '*Regain*' means the grass that grows after being cut, symbolic of the possibility in nature for rebirth.

There is some good Provençal detail in the film: young Gaubert and wife (Milly Mathis, who plays Fanny's buxom aunt in *Fanny*) arguing about the added cost of housing his father – to the old man's humiliation; Panturle offending his friend L'Amoureux by offering to pay for a loaf of bread which is meant as a gift; Fernandel's agonized 'Aïe-aïe-aïe' every time a new turn of fate threatens his solitary, petty-minded existence; the wearisome trudge of Gédémus and Arsule on the hilly road from Banon to Sault where Arsule wishes they could turn towards the sea because 'it's downhill'.

The whole, however, seems too heavy-handed, the message too obvious for a Pagnol picture. The actors playing Panturle and the old witch Mamèche were not part of the 'family'. And Pagnol does not seem at ease in the opening up of an intimate novel of great economy. What seems simple and subtle on the page comes out as pretentious and obvious on the screen. The clash of symbols is even louder than Honegger's strident, doom-laden score.

Uneasy about *Regain* but sure of his star, Pagnol shrewdly made a commercial vehicle for Fernandel in the same year (1937). He shot the two films simultaneously: *Regain* in good weather on location; *Le Schpountz* in bad weather at the studios. Understandably, Fernandel sometimes forgot which part he was playing. *Le Schpountz* also had a location that is an existing landmark near Aubagne, a tatty but charming *alimentation-tabac*, still with its original faded blue awning and shutters, where you can buy anything from Gauloises to grapes, and Fernandel served his famous 'anchovies fresh from the tropics'.

A '*schpountz*' was the private name, invented by Pagnol's East European cameraman, Willy, for the fans who plagued their locations and got in the way of his shots. They were as frustrating as the high-summer cicadas in the Vallon de Marcellin, chirruping over dialogue, were for the soundman.

In a wacky comedy of social manners, Fernandel plays a *schpountz*, a screen-struck Provençal grocer's nephew, who becomes embroiled with a Parisian film unit. The *schpountz* reckons he has a God-given talent as an actor, and the film crew play a mean trick on him, presenting him with a phoney contract. He duly presents himself at the Paris studios – with

Opposite: The alimentation-tabac at Eoures – the village store used by Marcel Pagnol in his film of Le Schpountz, *starring Fernandel.*

resulting near-disaster and humiliation. Pagnol, whose writing could be hilariously cruel at times, was nevertheless too shrewd to give a star vehicle an unhappy ending. By a twist of fate, their joke backfires on the film crew and their *schpountz* becomes a star – as a Napoleonic general – and returns in triumph to his uncle's shop in Eoures.

After this unabashed frolic, Pagnol took another Giono original off the back burner where it had been simmering for five years. It was to be one of his definitive movies, *La Femme du Boulanger* (1938).

Holed up in an end-of-season hotel near the rugged mountains of the Vercors, north of Provence, Pagnol was going through an emotional turmoil when he began work on the script.

The people of La Treille were used to Marcel's rapid turnover of female company. When he was making *Cigalon*, a ravishing secretary from his Paris office, Yvonne Pouperon, was the latest. Known as Vonette, she was a popular, high-spirited girl from Madagascar – in the Pagnol mould of girls from across the sea (Kitty from London and Orane from Algeria). Whatever madness took Marcel, she went with it. Everyone loved Vonette. In 1935 she had a daughter by him, Francine. Then suddenly she faded from Marcel's life as Kitty had done.

At Villard-de-Lans during his writing stint, extending Jean Giono's fifteen-page story to a full-length screenplay, Marcel was accompanied by Orane Demazis and their son, Jacques. As anyone who has spent a holiday with a workaholic writer knows, you also spend it with the writing. Marcel and Orane quarrelled. He was a man of the Midi, expecting a certain undemanding presence from the opposite sex; but Orane was no chattel, she had already made her own life as an actress. And not just a Pagnolian actress, either. Marcel could be an obsessive dreamer, lost in his own world, going his own way. The other was an appendage, required to put up with both his black moods of self-doubt and his success-driven ego. Women often had to take second place to his men friends, and always to his work meetings.

Charming and generous as he could be, Marcel also had a darker side, shared by many who have started life relatively poor: he was mistrustful. Women, he sometimes imagined, were after his money. In *La Prière aux Étoiles*, an unfinished film (1941), a character says: 'I once knew a woman who, after an hour's intimacy, wanted a rabbit coat, an afternoon gown, and an evening dress. Because I'd seen her naked for five minutes, I was supposed to dress her for life.'

Orane was not after his money. She may have been after marriage, as much for the sake of their son as herself. But Marcel was still officially married to Simonne. Enough was enough for both of them, and what was to be one of Pagnol's happiest films began badly. Evidence of his devotion to duty, if not to Orane, was that the script took only fifteen days to complete.

Giono's short fable about the Bread of Life and its importance to the Provençal village of Corbières was based on the Helen of Troy legend. The baker's wife is swept away by a handsome Piedmont shepherd to an island in the marshes of the Durance valley. The 'Trojan' villagers set out and fetch her back, as the baker can no longer bake without her. 'Love is all very well,' says Giono's village spokesman, 'but we've got to eat.'

In Provence women were expected to show a certain modesty; when Giono's Aurélie, the baker's wife, discovers the havoc that 'the odour of women' at a hot harvest can wreak on a man, her modesty is abandoned for the sensuality of another world. She is swept up to the stars in a cosmic movement both violent and tender, and may never come back.

Pagnol has been accused, by Giono supporters, of changing the emphasis of the story from the baker's wife to the baker, in order to make a tear-jerking star vehicle for Raimu. Such intellectual snobbery shows ignorance of the different requirements of literature and cinema. Film-making is an aleatory medium, with frequent changes of direction.

What Pagnol originally thought would be a short film had grown, in its natural development, to feature-length. His first

Baker Aimable (Raimu) serving a customer at his boulangerie in La Femme du Boulanger, *written and directed by Marcel Pagnol, based on Jean Giono's story (1938).*

casting idea for the baker was Maupi, the pot-bellied little ferryboat driver in *The Marseilles Trilogy*, but he was just not box-office enough for a full-length feature. So, with some qualms after their meridional slanging matches on *César*, he approached Raimu. Raimu, typically starry, said he had no intention of playing a part written for an underling like Maupi. In a rage, Pagnol offered the part to his faithful Henri Poupon, who wept with delight. He even had his teeth fixed to give himself a more baker-ish smile.

As for the baker's wife, who had to be sensual but subtly so, no French actress came readily to Pagnol's mind. Somebody suggested Joan Crawford. Pagnol liked the idea. She was beautiful and she played *femmes fatales*. She also did not speak a word of French. Pagnol reduced her spoken text to forty-four words.

Then, furious that his dangerously upcoming rival, Henri Poupon, was to play Aimable, Raimu came back fighting. Deviously, he suggested Ginette Leclerc, whom Pagnol had overlooked. She was a specialist in playing *femmes fatales*. Raimu had made her believe he was the lead, and she told Pagnol, in no uncertain terms, that she had no intention of playing Henri Poupon's wife.

The cinema was going through one of its perennial rough passages: Pagnol would be crazy not to take Raimu, advisers said. Friends and 'family' pressured him into dumping poor Poupon and his beautiful new teeth. It was one of the hardest letters Pagnol ever had to write. Such disloyalty to a friend, under commercial and artistic pressure, was hateful for him; for Poupon it was devastating.

Raimu, meticulous artist that he was, studied his new trade with M. Revest, a baker friend at his home town, Bandol. He adopted M. Revest's ruffled hairstyle, and borrowed M. Revest's bonnet and waistcoat and every gesture. He made M. Revest's domain his own.

> Those big round loaves, beautifully lined up, looked like a fortification. Then underneath, fancy breads; there was long bread and twin-headed bread which was made of two crispy balls joined by a thin strip; there were *fougasses* which looked rather like golden grilles, and soft little curly buns for breakfast, with an anchovy and an onion; on the counter, loaves brown as gypsies because they'd been twice through the oven: thanks to the baker's thoughtfulness, they were light as rusks for the delicate stomachs of old ladies

and for M. le Curé's dunking fingers (*Le Boulanger Amable*).

Corbières in the Durance valley, where the original Giono story took place, would have been too outlandish a location for the film. Pagnol decided La Treille was getting over-familiar to his audience, so settled for the hilltop village of Le Castellet which, besides being unspoilt in those days, was conveniently close to Raimu's seaside villa, La Ker Mocotte, at Bandol.

Raimu was delighted. The sacred monster took over the film. Pagnol had confidence in him, and returned for every take to the sound van, where he listened to dialogue rather than watching from behind the camera. 'In the beginning was the Word . . .' had been engraved on Pagnol's heart.

A medieval gateway at Le Castellet, seen in the opening sequence of La Femme du Boulanger.

One of the film's most effective scenes, however, happens in silence – a rarity in Pagnol's work.

The erotic mood is established as the marquis's handsome shepherd, Dominique, waits to pick up the bread. The bakery cat, Pomponette, having left her regular tom, Pompon, roams over the sacks of flour. Aurélie slowly puts the long, phallic loaves into Dominique's bread sack which he holds open. Her hair brushes his face as she counts the loaves. He is intoxicated with 'the odour of women'. She puts her hand in his shirt and whispers. . .

Emotions are also expressed comically, as when the cuckolded Aimable drowns his sorrows for the first time in his blameless life. Taking exception to the Curé's sermon in which his plight is treated as a useful moral lesson for the villagers' transgressions, he gets plastered on Pernod. As they return from Mass, his customers hear him singing self-mocking Piedmontese words about *lo boulangièro* whose *bella femma* ran off with her *bergièro*. And he swears he will bake not another loaf until she returns.

The Mayor, to avert the bread crisis, calls for village solidarity. In rising to thank them, Aimable is very careful of the lamp above him: 'I don't want to break it with my horns!' Everyone applauds his brave joke. He goes on: 'I don't know what I'm doing any more. So I'm scared of making you bread with sawdust without noticing it, or kneading your brioches with disinfectant. But if you bring me back my Aurélie, if you dispel my doubts, then you'll have a real baker. I'll bake you bread like you've never seen.'

When Aurélie returns, the final scene shows Pagnol at his best, balancing on a razor's edge of true sentiment that could so easily have been merely lachrymose. Aimable has prepared supper for her: a roast chicken, a bottle of wine, and bread in the shape of a heart. At first he pretends he believes she was at her mother's. She senses he knows the truth. He has started to bake again, but. . .

The Curé (Robert Vattier) and the Marquis (Fernand Charpin) gather outside the boulangerie (La Femme du Boulanger, *1938).*

Aurélie: Aimable, kindness like yours is worse than being beaten with a stick.
Aimable: (*kneading the dough*) So what? Kindness is difficult to hide. Excuse me. I didn't show it on purpose.
Aurélie: You know everything?
Aimable: Me? Yes. Everything about bread. And that's

enough for me. I don't want to know about anything else. How would that help me?

Aurélie: Not to look ridiculous.

(*He gets up and takes a step towards her. He is pale.*)

Aimable: So you don't want me to look ridiculous?

Aurélie: No.

Aimable: Those are the first and only words of love you've ever spoken to me. Now I don't know what to do.

But the return of the cat, Pomponette, from her lover gives him his chance. Every mean name he could have called Aurélie he now calls Pomponette: 'Bitch! Slut! Garbage! So now you're back? And poor Pompon's been pining for you these three days!'

The baker's oven went out when his wife left; it will start baking again now she's returned. Together Aimable and Aurélie relight the oven. As it always does, the smoke brings tears to his eyes.

La Femme du Boulanger began its triumphant screenings at the inauguration of Pagnol's own cinema, Le César, in Marseilles. His own Studios Marcel Pagnol were now open on Avenue Jean-Mermoz, and he had an apartment in the buildings. His base in Provence seemed secure, and his future as an independent French movie-maker never more rosy.

Success is a lawyers' hunting-ground. Jean Giono sued Pagnol for usurping rights in the publication of screenplays. His claim to have written screenplays himself without payment or credit was thrown out of court. And all he regained, after four years, was ownership of the title *La Femme du Boulanger.*

Although theirs was never truly a collaboration, this was a sad end to what had begun so fruitfully. Now, in search of a follow-up for the Raimu hit, Pagnol decided to go for an original of his own, *La Fille du Puisatier.* 'The Well-Digger's Daughter' had the same earthy, Provençal resonance as 'The Baker's Wife'.

During the Phoney War of 1940, Marcel met the well-known actress Josette Day. A classic, passionate night on the Blue Train from Paris to Cannes developed into one of the great loves of his life. Famous for her one-night stands, Josette seemed to have been tamed by Marcel. And she reformed his sloppy dress style: no more open-neck shirts but Charvet ties; hand-made shoes instead of espadrilles; even a change of underpants every day – which made Raimu break up with laughter.

He agreed, however, to play the well-digger in the new film,

with Josette Day as his daughter. He also agreed to share top
billing with Fernandel, probably because the now vastly
popular horse-faced actor was only the *assistant* well-digger –
another of his catalyst roles.

In fact, Pagnol unashamedly repeated himself, barely
disguising the maritime tale of *The Marseilles Trilogy* in country
clothing: boy-meets-girl, boy-leaves-girl, girl-has-baby, boy-
returns-to-girl. The recurring theme in Pagnol's love stories is
the clash between young lovers and traditional family values. If
the treatment sometimes resembles a nineteenth-century
novelette, as in *La Fille du Puisatier*, the contemporary
Provençal setting is authentic, in this case showing the
increasing encroachment of the Second World War on the lives
of ordinary French people.

The wartime love-child of Patricia, the well-digger's daughter,
was like the GI babies in Britain or wherever rude soldiery were
rampant and lonely. Contraception was unheard of in France,
except by natural means. Abortion was a mortal sin – and still is
amongst devout Catholics. Having a child out of wedlock could
be, even then, a statement of a woman's independence rather
than a burden of her sin.

Pagnol, with his contradictory Provençal nature – sometimes
macho, sometimes feminist – sympathetically portrayed another
heroine who, however submissive she might seem, survives a
conspiracy of men of so-called honour and morally virtuous
older women. Setting his morality tale in such a smugly pleasant
provincial town as Salon-de-Provence only underlined the
conflict. At the outbreak of the Second World War, Salon was
depicted as authentically as the claustrophobic, judgemental
little world of Flaubert's Normandy. And no one was more of a
spiritual Madame Bovary than Pagnol's own current love,
Josette Day.

The interminable twists and turns of the plot are relieved
by some nicely observed moments: Patricia bringing her father
and his assistant a good *daube* for lunch, served on a check
tablecloth even in the depths of the country where they are
blasting a well; France falling to the Nazis, and Maréchal
Pétain's grim speech heard on the radio by stunned Salonais,
Madame Mazel bitter that her son Jacques has died for
nothing; and the class conflict expressed between Pascal, the
well-digger, and Mazel, the storekeeper. Pascal says, 'Never
trust people who sell tools but don't know how to use them.'
His meridional sexism is demonstrated when, as the father of
five daughters, he tells his assistant, Félipe, how he longed for
a son.

Pascal: When the child was born, the women called
me and I went running, and they showed me
the baby: it was red as a crayfish ready to eat.
And I was happy. Then – *Ah! Malheur!* – I
saw it had no little prick. *Ah! Malheur!* I was
not happy.

Félipe: Why? A girl is pretty, too.

Pascal: Pretty, perhaps. But before they're married,
you don't know their name.

The success of *La Fille du Puisatier*, as a wartime morale-booster, added to Marcel Pagnol's prestige and wealth. But he did not, as they say, have a good war. It had started promisingly. The film industry was booming. During the Occupation Marseilles became, for a time, the capital of France. Cultural refugees like Jean Cocteau, Louis Jouvet, Max Ernst, André Breton and Tristan Tzara appeared; passing through were many others – Maurice Chevalier, Edith Piaf, Charles Trenet. And further along the coast at Sanary, a colony of refugees from Nazi Germany included Bertolt Brecht, Kurt Weill, and Thomas Mann.

With such talent concentrated within easy reach of his film studios, Marcel Pagnol – with characteristic pragmatism – set about creating a Hollywood-en-Provence. Then the Germans occupied southern France, too, and the talent dispersed – some to concentration camps, others to the long established Hollywood. The Germans begged Pagnol to continue to make morale-boosting movies for the French, but he flatly rejected this attempt to colonize the French film industry.

No bread, no circuses. Pagnol sold up. The sale of his Marseilles studios and other film interests went to pay for a 313-acre agricultural property at La Gaude, near Nice (the Pagnol family still owns the house and twelve acres). Some dozen members of his crew and studio staff could thus be employed on the land, which prevented them from being deported to German labour camps. Pagnol himself worked as a forester, and was spared further harassment from the Nazis for his refusal to work for them. Heroics were not for him: like Félipe in *La Fille du Puisatier*, '. . . to be a hero, it's not enough to have courage: you also have to have the chance – and as for me, I never had the chance.'

PAGNOL'S PROVENCE

Haute-Provence and the **Plateau de Vaucluse** are at their best with a lavish carpeting of spring flowers or in the greens and golds of autumn. Start at **Manosque**, home town of Jean Giono, where the agricultural fair in *Regain* took place (actually shot at Gémenos near Aubagne). The church clock could be seen from the farm by Angèle, aged six; here Jofroi bought his trees, and here Aimable had been baker before coming to the village.

You enter the old town of Manosque by the medieval Porte Saunerie. The belltower with the clock Angèle read belongs to the church of St-Sauveur; it can be seen from a little square where the only café serves delicious freshly ground coffee. Near the Place Marcel Pagnol, where immigrant workers' children play, are shops selling Tunisian delicacies. The old town is a warren of narrow streets and tiny squares; its Place de l'Hôtel de Ville has fine carved wood doors.

An ex-baker, now an official at the Tourist Office, told me regretfully: 'After Aimable moved from Manosque, nobody took his place.' It was now bereft of artisanal bakeries, but at the Saturday market country people sell large, round loaves of *pain de campagne*, baked in their own wood-fired ovens. In this region, the nearest bakery to Aimable's for *bon vieux temps* ambience is at **Dauphin**, a perched village well worth the visit for its other charms. Outside the bakery, in a bower of flowers, is a table and chairs for tasting your *fougasse* with a cooling soft drink; it is also the village store.

On knife-grinder Gédémus's itinerary in *Regain* was **Forcalquier**, one of my favourite small towns in this part of France. Its life is concentrated around one square in the centre of town, the Place de Bourguet: the Bar Bourguet Sport, with its huge, colourful poster for the locally made liqueur, Rinquinquin; the cathedral, Notre Dame du Marché; and a cinema in the seventeenth-century chapel of Les Visitandines convent. If you're feeling energetic, a climb to the citadel is well rewarded with views of Pagnol–Giono country.

Life on the land has changed since Giono wrote of its hardships; the area no longer looks neglected and even appears prosperous with its spruce olive groves, rolling green fields and dazzling sunflowers.

The road north to **Banon** is the Route de Lavande, with huge crumbling, isolated farms like the Ferme d'Angèle amid the lavender and cornfields. A detour to the summit of **La Montagne de Lure** (5,863 feet) is a gentle climb through cedar forests; skiing in winter, magnificent views south to the Lubéron, west to Mont Ventoux, east to the Durance valley, and north to the Alps. Alpine flowers abound, as do eminently filmable sunsets.

Banon gives its name to a famous goat's cheese wrapped in vine leaves. At the top of the town is an imposing gatehouse for dropping hot lead on a medieval enemy. The Rue des Arcades has a number of bridge houses, including a fine Renaissance one.

On the road to **Sault**, take another detour to **La Contadour**, a village where Jean Giono founded an ill-fated back-to-nature community. A centre of wartime Resistance activities, it stands in a gentle fold of the land in the shadow of La Montagne de Lure. Its chapel, which is being restored, has some good modern stained glass.

On the way through wild, gorse-yellow highlands, you pass a sign announcing the village of **Redortiers**, but there's only a tower and archway of it left, perched on a terraced hill. Inhabited as late as the nineteenth century, its desertion inspired Jean Giono to write *Regain*.

The Gendarmerie of Sault is where Gédémus was held for the suspected murder of Arsule. It also has the best nougat in France chez Boyer.

Best bet is to arm yourself with the *Gîtes de France* guide to Bed & Breakfasts and Ferme–Auberges, where you're more likely to meet Pagnol fans and critics, eat local produce, and feel more part of the country than in a hotel.

The Domaine d'Aurouze (moderate) at St-Martin-les-Eaux is an eighteenth-century *bastide* with music room and library, and good food. Near Manosque is Les Cigales (inexpensive), if you just want B & B.

Also near Manosque is the celebrated Hostellerie de la Fuste (expensive), luxury in a peaceful Provençal garden, rating one Michelin star for its local truffle dishes, milk-fed Sisteron lamb and local game. Jugged hare and wild boar are on many menus during the hunting season – at the Restaurant Signoret (inexpensive) in Sault, for example.

Forcalquier has the Hostellerie des Deux Lions (moderate), which also boasts one Michelin star for its rather more elaborate but reasonably priced food. Régusse is a very drinkable local wine.

At Banon I had the unusual experience of being welcomed for lunch at 2.15 by the Patronne of L'Hôtel des Voyageurs (inexpensive), and very good it was, too.

The esplanade of **La Treille**, used in *Jofroi*, the Cigalon restaurant, and the *alimentation-tabac* at **Eoures** (*Le Schpountz*) can all be seen during your Aubagne stay (see pages 23–7). Likewise **Les Barres de St-Esprit** and the **Vallon de Marcellin**, with their vestiges of Mius Brouquier's location buildings for *Regain* and *Angèle*. The well still stands, like a

Overleaf: Dawn over the Durance valley, where the baker's wife and her lover hide away for their brief idyll in La Femme du Boulanger.

stone beehive. Sadly, there is not much else left of Mius's work. For years his location buildings have been *chefs d'oeuvre en peril* (threatened works of art), as the French rightly call crumbling historic sites. And if the Ferme d'Angèle, where the heroine hid with her baby, was not exactly Chenonceaux, it would be good to see more of it than a few old stones.

A climb to inspect the archway and Panturle's house was well rewarded by a bird's-eye view of La Treille, a panorama of the hills, and Marseilles in a classic clear sunrise before the pall of smog envelops it when the morning rush hour gets under way.

The coastal village of **Le Castellet**, where Pagnol made *La Femme du Boulanger*, was a medieval stronghold. You can still walk through Le Portalet, a small gateway in the ramparts, seen in the opening sequence. The school on the Place de l'Ormeau is now closed, but the gnarled elm tree gives delightful shade on a blistering day. And the fortified church where Aimable takes such exception to the Curé's sermon is another cool spot.

As for the rest of the present village, it is tarted-up Provençal at its worst, over-restored for mass tourism with souvenir shops of Parfums de Provence and rétro Marseilles posters. Outside La Dame de Castellet, a pottery shop which was once Aimable's bakery, a vast ceramic tortoise waits for a buyer.

Cider and pancakes are available at the Roy d'Ys crêperie of the Auberge Castellane; the acacia and micocoulier trees on its terrace rustled too loudly in the mistral and made Raimu forget his lines in the famous drunk scene. It eventually had to be shot in a Marseilles studio replica of the location.

To find an artisanal, wood-fired baker's oven in Provence is getting harder and harder. Besides the one already mentioned at Dauphin, with its encouraging sign '*Pain au levain cuit au bois*', La Gloriette at Merindol-les-Oliviers near Vaison-la-Romaine provides traditional Provençal breads like *fougasse* (grille-shaped), breads made with olives, onion, bacon bits, whole wheat, bran, and a local grain called *épeautre*.

Raimu's villa at **Bandol** on the coast is now a hotel, the Villa Ker Mocotte. It is pleasant to have a drink on the terrace, overlooking a little bay. Bandol makes one of the best wines in the region on its steep terraces, so don't miss a tasting, preferably at Domaine Tempier or Domaine Ott.

Salon-de-Provence, scene of La Fille du Puisatier, is the birthplace of the medieval astrologer-physician Nostradamus and the contemporary pop singer, Mireille Mathieu.

The vast, blocky, gold stone church of St-Laurent with its ornate nineteenth-century gilded statue of the Virgin outside provides a spacious tryst for secret lovers like Patricia and Jacques. Pagnol made Jacques a fighter pilot, using the nearby air base which still exists. But in those days, couples from different strata of society, like Jacques and Patricia, would not have been seen together at the pleasant cafés by the mossy fountain of the Place Crousillat; nor strolling hand in hand through the magnificent seventeenth-century Porte de L'Horloge to the Renaissance Château Empéri, now famous for its music festival.

Three miles out of town is the Abbaye de Sainte-Croix (expensive), offering delicious breast of pigeon with Bandol wine and nineteen very comfortable rooms. Devem de Mirapier (moderate) is another pleasant country stopover.

CHAPTER SIX

LAST
LAUGHS

*The Bay of Cassis, where the Rostaings
in* Naïs, *and Panisse and Fanny in*
The Marseilles Trilogy, *have seaside villas.*

'*L*aughter is a human thing . . . a virtue belonging only to Man and which God has perhaps given him as a consolation for being intelligent' (*Le Schpountz*). In the latter part of the Marcel Pagnol story, laughs were kept light and tears not too bitter by a change of direction in his haphazard love life.

At fifty, he married an actress in her early twenties from southern France. She was to remain his wife for life, accompanying him on a roller-coaster of success and failure, through to his acceptance, comparatively late in his career, as an important figure on the French literary scene.

Jacqueline Bouvier, a civil servant's daughter, was born in Ribaute-les-Tavernes near Nîmes. Although strictly Languedocienne, she had looked after a herd of goats in the Camargue as a child – and that was good enough for Marcel: despite her fair-skinned northern beauty and lack of a Midi accent, she was Provençal to him. She did not have to pronounce *enfin* as *unfung* or Fanny as *Fannee* to convince him.

As a teenage schoolgirl Jacqueline had walked into Marcel's Paris office in Rue Fortuny for an audition, and had quite taken his mind off his anxieties over some later-to-be-forgotten project. Although her sunny disposition reminded Marcel of what he was missing in the grey of Paris, his meridional blood remained cool. He took her out to dinner a couple of times, and she recited him a poem she had written. That's as far as it went.

Now, in 1944, she had bloomed into an actress as bright as she was beautiful and was reading Alfred Jarry's poetry in an avant-garde Paris cabaret. She had made a name for herself in a Simenon movie, amongst others; she had partnered Charles Trenet. And Marcel, meeting her again after a particularly bitter break-up with Josette Day, found her just the post-war tonic he needed: a beautiful Midi girl, quick to laugh, restoring his faith in women. As he wrote to Jean Cocteau: 'She has saved me from black moods, meanness, and pessimism.'

Naïs was their first project together, with Jacqueline playing the title role. Once again he would surround himself with 'family' – and in roles they were already familiar with: Poupon's Micoulin was another angry farmer, like his Clarius in *Angèle*; Fernandel was to play his third Pagnol go-between, this time the embittered hunchback, Toine; Blavette's never-failing 'best friend' reappeared as Henri; and had he been alive, Charpin would surely have been cast as the Aix lawyer, Rostaing (played by Arius), a slightly more upmarket clone of Mazel in *La Fille du Puisatier*.

The 'new boy' this time was the raffishly Provençal *jeune premier*, Raymond Pellegrin, excellent as the wild-living law student, Rostaing's son Frédéric, reformed – more or less – by love for the farmer's daughter, Naïs.

In 1877 Aix-born Émile Zola wrote a short novel, *Naïs Micoulin*, at the fishing village of L'Estaque, just north of Marseilles. His old schoolfriend Paul Cézanne painted there, and it was later to become a colony of Fauves artists – Matisse, Dufy and Derain. Although Pagnol didn't know Zola's Mediterranean story when it was brought to him, the elements instantly appealed to him: conflict between bourgeoisie and workers, town and country; heightened emotions; a strong love story; opportunities for comedy of manners. Also, he would return to a setting he had used only once before, the Mediterranean coast of *César*, plus an entirely new setting in Aix-en-Provence, which he had known since his days as a schoolmaster there.

The hunchback Toine doesn't dare declare his love to Naïs, and is bitter when, as a maid at the Rostaing villa, she has an affair with Frédéric. But he acts the good fairy, protecting her from the wrath of her father, Micoulin, who tries to murder Frédéric. Toine gets in first by killing Micoulin in 'an unfortunate accident', and gets Micoulin's job as caretaker of the villa.

In one of the film's best scenes, Toine asks Madame Rostaing to take Naïs as a maid to Aix; there's no future for her here, as a hunchback's farmgirl. 'You go on too much about your hump,' Madame Rostaing says.

Toine explains why. His grandmother used to encourage him when he was a child, by singing a song: 'Little hunchbacks are little angels, who hide their wings under their overcoats. That's the secret of little hunchbacks. . .' But, he adds, grandmothers are like mimosa, they're soft and cool and fragile. One day his grandmother was no longer there. And a little hunchback without a grandmother's comforting songs, he soon found out, was no angel.

Thanks to Fernandel's ability to play for truth rather than sentiment, his Quasimodo is never mawkish. And Pagnol always gives him good jokes. This is how he deals with Micoulin's threat to do away with the lovers: 'Frankly, all we have to do is kill him!' (*He looks at Naïs who says nothing.*) 'Since he's told you he would kill himself *after*, it would be better to kill him *before*. . .'(*Naïs still says nothing.*) 'That way, he won't have committed a crime . . . it would be doing him a favour!'

Whether or not the lawyer Frédéric flouted stuffy Aix convention and married his mother's chambermaid Naïs, we shall never know.

Marcel and Jacqueline were married in Paris in 1945. His divorce from Simonne Collin had come through in 1941, but he was hesitant to commit himself again. His caution had paid off with Josette Day. He already had three children by other women; he was to have two more with Jacqueline, a son Frédéric and daughter Estelle. Sadly, Estelle died, aged two.

Sudden bereavement had been his lot four times: his mother; his childhood friend, Lili; his brother, Paul; and now his daughter, Estelle. It affected him deeply. Like many artists, he was prey to extreme mood swings, often seeking escape from despair in some new, therapeutic project.

In the latter part of his life, Pagnol spent more and more time with Jacqueline in Paris; his last home, where Madame Pagnol still lives, was a house in the exclusive Square de l'Avenue Foch, surrounded by chestnut trees and the sound of his neighbour, Artur Rubinstein, practising the piano. Pagnol found Provence too distracting for work. A sumptuous home, La Lestra, in what he called 'provincial' Monte Carlo, was swiftly sold after the death of Estelle there. Only the property at La Gaude remained.

The spectre of has-been haunted him. 'He has nothing more to say' proclaimed the bitchy Paris glitterati, who relished failure like a meal at Maxim's. But somehow, Marcel Pagnol always did have something more to say. The critic Jean-Jacques Gautier described him as 'an anxious optimist'.

Life was a mixture, as so often with ageing celebrities, of honours and dishonours. In 1947 he was the first cinéaste to be elected to the Académie Française, France's most illustrious body of *intellos*. In a photograph, he wears the green, gold-braided uniform, sprouting medals, with just a hint of irony in the proud smile. He wrote to a friend saying that he hardly dared put pen to paper any more for fear of making a spelling mistake. In an interview he talked about the Academy: 'I find it very pleasant there, meeting celebrated writers or sages who talk as though they were not.'

Plaudits came from other international pace-makers in the film industry like Roberto Rossellini and Orson Welles. And yet a theatre revival of *Marius* flopped, as did *La Belle Meunière*, a movie operetta with Tino Rossi as Franz Schubert, shot at a mill near Colle-sur-Loup in the hills behind Antibes which were meant to be the Austrian Tyrol. It was a fatal mish-mash, filmed using a new colour process which added to Pagnol's problems.

After the death of Joseph Pagnol in 1951, Pagnol returned to the land of his forebears to work on the film of *Manon des Sources*. Even in the terrible but appropriate drought of 1952, filming in the desert heat of sun-scorched hills, he was creatively safer on his home ground.

The final version was cut down from four hours to three hours ten minutes. It is a measure of the public's fidelity to Pagnol's Provence that they would sit through and mostly enjoy an epic of *Gone With the Wind* proportions about water. Later, as Pagnol intended, it became two films, *Manon des Sources* and *Ugolin*, and this version can now be obtained in the Collection Marcel Pagnol video series produced by the Compagnie Méditerranéenne de Films.

In his return to what he knew best – the force of destiny at work in the hills of his youth – Pagnol evoked the suffering of people faced with lack of water in that hard, arid hinterland. The sight of a nearly empty water tank or a spring's abundance reduced to a trickle strikes fear into the hearts of the strongest. By May, most wells are dry. As Marcel's childhood friend, Lili des Bellons, had told him: a spring is often a peasant's closely guarded secret that can die with him.

After the non-productive years of the Occupation and a

Jacqueline Pagnol, Marcel's actress wife, as Manon *in* Manon des Sources, *the first version written and directed by Pagnol (1952).*

number of post-war flops, the filming at La Treille and the surrounding hills gave Pagnol, then approaching sixty, a new zest for life. Jacqueline Pagnol, as Manon, had just the right wild blondness for the girl of the hills who takes her revenge on a whole village. His now vast family lived in a La Treille villa, La Pascaline. He was surrounded by 'members of the club': the long-suffering cameraman, Willy, by now used to long trudges into outlandish places with heavy equipment; and the actors, like a travelling company who'd been together for years – Henri Poupon, Charles Blavette, Edouard Delmont, Milly Mathis and Robert Vattier.

In 1954 he turned to another Provençal project, a sketch film of four Alphonse Daudet stories in *Letters from My Windmill*. Marius Brouquier reconstructed the author's famous Fontvieille windmill on one of the Étoile hills, La Tête Ronde. The windmill's sails turned a good deal more smoothly than the camera; although Daudet, like Mistral and Dickens, was one of Pagnol's favourite narrative masters, the film adaptation was a long four hours and, unlike *Manon des Sources*, impossible to cut down to a showable length satisfactorily. The décor had its usual impeccable authenticity, particularly the Abbey of St-Michel-de-Frigolet near Tarascon and the Priory of Ganagobie near Forcalquier for the 'Elixir du Père Gaucher' sequence.

At Ganagobie, Marcel's despondency was relieved by the friendly visit of Jean Giono. For some months – since Marcel had sponsored Jean's candidature for an important literary prize in Monaco – hard feelings over their law suit had been forgotten. After a riotous lunch of jokes and good conversation in one of the monks' cells, Marcel suggested it was high time that the French Academy was honoured by the presence of Jean Giono, whom he considered to be the greatest living French author. But Jean declined: Paris was not Manosque, and he did not relish visiting it more frequently – even for such a literary honour.

Les Lettres de Mon Moulin was Pagnol's last film.

Death on 18 April 1974, at the age of seventy-nine, followed a long illness. As befitted a Frenchman of such artistic achievement, Pagnol was given a red carpet send-off at the church of St-Honoré in the Place Victor-Hugo, Paris. Guards of honour presented arms, the Minister of Culture stood in for the President, and Pagnol's fellow members of the French Academy – known as 'the Immortals' – made an impressive showing in their uniforms and two-pointed hats.

Considerably less pomp and ceremony attended his burial at the cemetery of La Treille. Pagnol lies in a simple grave, without a cross out of respect for the laic convictions inherited from his father; he did, however, have Extreme Unction near the end of his life – possibly in memory of his devout mother who had him baptized without his father's knowledge.

By this time a Marseilles quay and a state-of-the-art Lycée in the St-Loup district had been named after him. And his childhood memoirs, *La Gloire de Mon Père* and *Le Château de Ma Mère*, entered the official college reading lists in France.

His international reputation had long been secure. By 1938 there were already Swedish and German films of *Marius*, an Italian film of *Fanny*, and Egyptian and Chinese films of *Topaze*. It was then MGM's turn: Preston Sturges, a great director of homely comedies with literate scripts, seemed perfect to remake *The Marseilles Trilogy* in one complete Hollywood movie starring Wallace Beery as César. Sturges had not only enticed Pagnol, financially embarrassed at the time, with big bucks for the rights but, more extraordinarily, had seduced the obdurate Hays Office into accepting a story centred on an illegitimate child.

In America, the unfortunately anatomical name of the heroine necessitated a change of title: *Fanny* became *Port of Seven Seas*. After receiving goodish notices, the film was mysteriously withdrawn from the circuit; perhaps the Hays Office had second thoughts.

The Abominable Showman David Merrick, never one to be afraid of censorship, critics, or even of actors who gave him a black eye, fearlessly kept the title *Fanny* for his 1954 Broadway hit. It even made a romantic song, ripe for hilarious parody. Director-librettist Joshua Logan went on to perpetrate the 1961 movie. The people of Marseilles laughed aloud when a trio of top Hollywood French paraded the quays of the Old Port in funny hats and with even funnier accents: Charles Boyer (César), Maurice Chevalier (Panisse), and Leslie Caron (Fanny). A German actor, Horst Buchholz, playing Marius, provoked a slightly more bitter laugh. The film, understandably, did not have its première in Marseilles.

Francophile Alan Jay Lerner, of *My Fair Lady* and *Gigi* fame, writes in his book *The Musical Theatre*:

> When I learned of it, I must confess it was one of the few times in my life when I was paralysed with envy . . . those three films were the finest subject matter for a musical invented by man . . . somewhere along the line a step was taken on to the wrong road, and the further they went the dimmer became the original goal.

Overleaf: Olive trees in the Durance valley.

One good song never makes a definitive musical. A sea of sentimentality swamped the sensuality of the original and sank the wit into the bargain. Pagnol's Provence, however, was by now an indestructible legend. Other directors and actors were to do it justice in the 1980s. And a musical of *Jean de Florette*, planned for London, is waiting in the wings.

Marcel Pagnol's epitaph for Raimu might have been written for him:

> Happily, films remain, so we may preserve your earthly reflection . . . you practise your art, you continue to follow your career, and today it is a measure of our gratitude to the magic lamp that it revives the light of extinguished genius, makes dead dancers dance again, and tenderly reminds us of the smile of lost friends.

PAGNOL'S PROVENCE

Pagnol was astute to keep Zola's **Aix-en-Provence** as the home of the Rostaings in *Naïs*. Aix flourished in the seventeenth and eighteenth centuries, when Louis XIV wisely allowed it to inaugurate its own Provençal law courts, of which the legal eagle Rostaings were the natural inheritors. It was the beginning of unprecedented prosperity. The Cours Mirabeau, arguably the most beautiful street in France, is lined with elegant mansions and shaded with plane trees, its pavement cafés like Les Deux Garçons vibrant with students from the university.

Passing tintinnabulous fountains, Frédéric would not have had far to walk to his home, probably in a quiet square like Place d'Albertas or a residential street like Rue Cardinale, which is near the Lycée Mignet where Marcel Pagnol once taught and Émile Zola went to school.

Zola's father was an engineer of Italian origin, and Émile would have been surrounded by Rostaings in his youth. He no doubt used them as models for his short novel, *Naïs Micoulin*. If Frédéric ever did get around to marrying the farmer's daughter Naïs, it would probably not have been at St-Sauveur's cathedral; Aix, for all its international festivals and cosmopolitan visitors of all social classes, is still the sort of city where like marry like, and even a Marseillais from a mere nineteen miles away is considered a dubious intruder.

While visiting Aix on the Pagnol trail, take in the Cézanne trail, too – his studio, the Granet Museum, the red-soiled countryside round Le Tholonnet, and La Montagne Ste-Victoire.

There is a good choice of hotels at Aix. For charm, I recommend Augustins (expensive to moderate), in a fifteenth-century convent just off the Cours (ask for a back room with terrace); Le Manoir (moderate) with useful courtyard parking – a hassle in mid-town; and La Cardinale (moderate), a friendly small hotel in Rue Cardinale. On the Cours Mirabeau, eat at Côté Cour (inexpensive). La Vieille Auberge (moderate), in a charming square just off the Place Jeanne d'Arc, serves *crespau provençal*, a regional speciality like a pepper and tomato omelette. Where the Rostaings would almost certainly have gone for family binges is Clos de la Violette (expensive) – Provençal haute-cuisine in beautiful if stuffy surroundings. Among the best Aixois wines are Châteaux Simone and Vignelaure.

The Rostaings had a holiday villa at **Cassis**, as did Fanny and Panisse. Still one of the most charming small coastal towns, though to be avoided in July and August, Cassis also makes a good, flinty white wine from its coastal vineyards, a perfect accompaniment to fish soup, *bourride*, and *bouillabaisse*. Clos de la Magdeleine is one of the best.

The bay is encompassed by high cliffs – Cap Canaille to the east, the Massif de Puguet to the west. Pagnol shot many of his exteriors on the pine-covered hill overlooking the bay, now occupied by a château owned by Michelin. However, a delightful walk up a lane between walled gardens, reminiscent of the Provençal road described in *La Gloire de Mon Père*, takes one to a short stretch open to the sea. Near an Aleppo pine sticking out from the cliff, the port and beach of Cassis can be seen much as the Rostaing family saw it from their secluded luxury.

Boules is a serious sport on the port and it is fun to watch the players in front of the Hôtel Liautaud. There is much shaking of hands, gesticulating, patting backs, swinging the ball when taking aim – an endless movement of arms. Marcel Pagnol, a teacher of English, found it hard actually to talk to the English in their own language because they never used their hands.

The Hôtel Liautaud (inexpensive) is conveniently on the port but noisy at night. Quieter and more luxurious is Les Roches Blanches (moderate to expensive), perched out on the rocks, as its name suggests, with excellent swimming. Avoid the waterfront restaurants except La Vieille Auberge and Nino (moderate). La Presqu'île (moderate) is a great place to watch the sunset on the cliffs of Cap Canaille which seem to change colour every second.

The port of Cassis is where boats leave for the clear, emerald

waters of **Les Calanques**, creeks which are a paradise for divers, rock-climbers, or just beach lizards in search of natural surroundings. There are next to no buildings, just pine-covered *barres* and towering cliffs of grey, blue, green and reddish rock, often in strange shapes like Egyptian mummies, crocodiles, dromedaries, their sheer face scored and scarred by time and the weather, and punctuated by 'windows' and climbers' 'chimneys'.

Unbelievable as it may sound on the French Riviera, there are still small communities who live in cabins with no electricity or drinking water.

Les Calanques feature in both *César* and *Naïs*. We saw a lot more of them from the *Esther III*, which took us first to the main three: Port-Miou, a long, thin, winding marina; Port-Pin, a paradise of grey rocks, pines and clear, green water; and En Vau, Provençal for 'in the valley' – and that's what it feels like, a spectacular meeting of sea and mountain, towering cliffs falling sheer into the calmest, most sheltered of waters. We continued to Morgiou, a tiny fishing village, and returned by way of the smaller creeks, each with its own weird rock formations and name – Sugiton, Oeil de Verre, Devenson, Loule.

This is where the rockfish, essential to a real *bouillabaisse*, come from. Pagnol, usually allergic to the sea, used to enjoy fishing from Les Roches Blanches.

Opposite: Early morning at a café on the Cours Mirabeau, the main street of Aix-en-Provence, the city where Marcel Pagnol was once a schoolmaster and which is the setting for scenes in the film Naïs.

Nowadays **L'Estaque**, where Pagnol wrote the screenplay of *Naïs* at the Château Fallet and where Toine worked at the brick factory, is a marina suburb near the port of Marseilles. But penetrate its winding back streets and you will find a church square where lively Pagnolian old men still sing Vincent Scotto's 'La Canebièr-e' and a flower-decked alley leads to a cottage where Cézanne once lived. They will tell you that a brick factory used to be where the church now stands. Believe it or not.

It's worth driving on towards the ominous grey mass of La Chaîne de L'Estaque to two spots mentioned briefly in *The Marseilles Trilogy*. **Niolon** is a tiny, ramshackle fishing village between desert-like hills. Its port is like a clear, sea-water swimming-pool, and La Pergola restaurant, overlooking it, offers very simple food at not so simple prices. Much more expensive is L'Escale at **Carry-le-Rouet**, which serves one of 'the best' *bouillabaisses* on the coast. Carry is where Pagnol's water-divining friend Abbé Cuque came from. L'Espace Fernandel, its art deco cinema, is named for the star because he had a holiday home here.

The **La Treille** cemetery, where Pagnol is buried, can either be visited on your Pagnolia trek (see pages 68–71) or separately by car. For the less energetic, a car can be driven beyond La Treille, as far as **La Bastide Neuve**, the Pagnol holiday home.

The cemetery has a peaceful setting against a backdrop of the lushly wooded Barres de St-Esprit, where Pagnol shot so many of his films. The epitaph on his grave reads 'He loved springs, his friends, and his wife'. Death, for the Pagnols, is very much a family affair. In the same tomb are buried his mother Augustine and his daughter Estelle; in another near by, father Joseph, brother Paul and stepmother Madeleine. Two friends who marked his life also lie near him: Marius ('Mius') Brouquier, master builder, who lived for seventy years in the same La Treille house, and was Marcel's right-hand man in location construction for his films; and his childhood 'little brother of the hills', Lili, whose name also appears on a La Treille church plaque as one of the 'Children of the Village Who Gave Their Lives For Their Country' in the First World War.

In his 1952 version of *Manon des Sources*, Pagnol used the village fountain. Also, a mile or so on your descent from **Le Garlaban**, a rusty signpost on your right points to **La Grotte de Manon**. A perilous path leads to the bottom of the **Vallon du Passe-Temps** and Manon's cave, otherwise known as La Grotte du Plantier. It was here that Pagnol decided Manon should live with her mother and the Piedmontese Baptistine after Jean de

Florette's death. From the craggy heights the rejected Ugolin emitted his crazed, desperate cries of 'Manon, I love you, I love you.'

Further down, on the Chemin de Ruissatel, is the little farmhouse that was Ugolin's **Mas de Massacan**.

One of the most spectacular places to visit in the Basses-Alpes is the **Prieuré de Ganagobie**, where Pagnol made his peace with Giono during the shooting of *Les Lettres de Mon Moulin*. Situated on a hill on the west side of the Durance valley between Volx and Peyruis, the Benedictine abbey (of the same period as Cluny) has just undergone a long and thorough restoration. The twelfth-century Romanesque church can be visited, but not the monastery.

In a lyrical setting of woodland and lavender, the church is at one end of a long avenue of trees leading to a belvedere with breathtaking views to the Alps and down to the curiously meandering Durance; its islands and marshes enticed Aurélie, the baker's wife, and Dominique to their short-lived idyll.

Having satisfied the spirit, satisfy the body at La Bonne Étape at Château-Arnoux (expensive). The Gleizes are charming hosts, and the food even better than the usually copious French film location lunch which Pagnol and Giono must have enjoyed at Ganagobie.

Also seen in *Les Lettres de Mon Moulin* is the abbey of St-Michel-de-Frigolet near **Tarascon**.

CHAPTER SEVEN

PAGNOL REVISITED

The garrigue *near Mont Cuques, where Claude Berri shot locations for* Jean de Florette *and* Manon des Sources.

*M*arcel Pagnol's work reflected a lifelong respect for the universality of previous Provençal authors like Alphonse Daudet and Frédéric Mistral. Witness this speech from his 1954 screenplay for Daudet's *Letters from My Windmill*:

> Whether you read Mistral's *Mireille* in Stockholm, Madrid or London, it's always the voice of Provence. . . If I could, I'd translate Mireille into Eskimo and read this great poem out loud . . . and they'd see, conjured up in the night, the mulberry trees of La Crau, the fig trees of the Camargue, the transhumance of sheep and the chapel of Saintes-Maries. . . The words are only a vehicle: when you want to travel, it's sensible to choose the one which goes fastest and furthest.

Pagnol put those words into the mouth of Alphonse Daudet, and they came from the heart. Translation into Eskimo may yet elude him, but his works have appeared in English, Spanish, German, Russian, Italian, Japanese, Chinese and many other languages. His childhood memoirs, *Souvenirs d'Enfance*, have sold over two and a half million copies throughout the world.

Such was the magnitude and inimitability of Pagnol's talent as a storyteller that no other film-maker had really done justice to his work until Claude Berri (and his co-writer, Gérard Brach) adapted *L'Eau des Collines* as a two-part film, *Jean de Florette*, and *Manon des Sources* in 1986.

Berri had the advantage of having 'the novel of the film' to work from. Typically, Pagnol had turned things on their head and, inspired to transfer celluloid into print, had transformed what is often a hack job into a literary masterpiece with *L'Eau des Collines*, first published in 1962. In his own film Pagnol had an early scene of exposition, when a retired village notary tells the tale of Manon's father, a hunchback called Jean de Florette. Pagnol found there was enough material in Manon's childhood for Part I of his novel, and later gave Berri the structure to which he adhered most faithfully.

The book of *Jean de Florette* begins with a long description of Les Bastides Blanches, a 150-inhabitant parish based on La Treille. It is as authentic as the true tale of springs which Pagnol remembered an Aubagne peasant telling him when he was in his early teens. Its inhabitants, though only twelve miles from Marseilles, could not be more different from César, Panisse, Escartefigue and Co. They are secretive, rarely venturing to the city, content with a weekly trip to the market or brothel in

Aubagne. In their proud isolation, they could be descended from the ancient cave-dwellers, *les pestiférés* – former coast-dwellers often unjustly thought to be infected by the plague and banished from the city to the hills.

There was a strict code of conduct. First rule: whatever tall stories you heard or told or relished about others, you never interfered with their business. Second rule: you were obliged to consider Les Bastides Blanches as the most beautiful village in Provence, far more important than neighbouring parishes like Les Ombrées and Ruissatel or, above all, the detested Crespin.

> As in all villages, there were jealousies, rivalries, and even long-standing hatreds stemming from stories of burned wills or land unfairly shared; but, in the event of attack from outside, like the intrusion of a poacher from Les Ombrées, or a mushroomer from Crespin, all the Bastidians rallied as one, ready to do common battle and bear collective false witness; and this solidarity was so strong that the Médérics, fighting for two generations with the baker's family, always bought their bread from him, but through sign language, never a spoken word. In fact, they lived in the hills, and the baker of Les Ombrées was nearer their farm. Nothing in the world, however, would have induced them to eat 'foreign' bread on the land of the commune.

The Mayor, Philoxène, owns the *bar-tabac*. He is socialist-laic-anticlerical and known as 'the Brain'. He has the village's only telephone. Natural selection has made him leader of a group of unbelievers who never go to Mass, preferring their regular Sunday game of *boules* or a long apéritif on the terrace. The baker's name is Martial, but everyone has forgotten it; he is simply 'the Baker'. The peasant Cabridan is known as 'the King of Chick Peas', because his are the biggest and best. The blacksmith, Casimir, has such hairy arms you can't see the skin.

These *notables*, of course, have wives. 'The women, beneath their flowery scarves, showed fine features, but had foreheads prematurely lined, hands dried up by gritty washing powder; their daughters, beneath hats loaded with flowers and sometimes fruit, were as beautiful as the girls of Arles.'

And scandal had struck, years ago, when one of the women of Les Bastides Blanches, Florette des Camoins, married Lionel Cadoret of Crespin. It implicated the Soubeyrans, the biggest and wealthiest landowners in the commune: César Soubeyran (known as Le Papet – grandfather or paterfamilias – although he was never married), at sixty still cuts a fine figure in spite of a twinge of rheumatism; he had once been Florette's lover.

It was the habit in such villages for sons to be known by the first name of their mother, rather than their family names: Pamphile de Fortunette, Clarius de Reine, Jean de Florette.

Claude Berri's film of *Jean de Florette*, dedicated to Marcel and Jacqueline Pagnol, begins with a bus driving at dawn through the *garrigue*-covered hills to Les Bastides Blanches. Ugolin has returned from military service in Antibes. As he passes the old house of the Soubeyrans which dominates the village, Le Papet welcomes his godson-nephew. Of Le Papet's four brothers, two died during the First World War and two killed themselves; Ugolin, his keen eyes glinting, is Le Papet's sole heir and his godfather has bought him the Mas de Massacan.

'Le Mas des Romarins' – the bastide near Riboux which played the part of the farm where Jean de Florette tried to make his dreams of country life come true, with disastrous results.

It was quite a long building, almost at the top of a hillside, in front of a thick pine wood, and just opposite Les Bastides, separated from it by a long, narrow valley.

Below the *mas*, terraced fields descended to the bottom of the hillside: they were strips of earth held up by dry stone walls. Dotted about were neatly pruned olive, almond and apricot trees and patches of tomatoes, maize and a little corn.

A rocky road went zigzagging up, and then disappeared into the Vallon des Romarins, further up in the
hills. Passing by the *mas* the road widened into an
esplanade, behind which the building stood, near a
well shaded by an old fig tree.

Thanks to this well, Ugolin cultivates carnations.

Le Papet lives in almost bourgeois style; he boasts a servant
and drinks good wine with his dinner. He betrays his peasant
origins only by wearing his hat indoors. Ugolin, he thinks,
should get married, but Ugolin is quite happy as a bachelor. His
carnations come first. But the well does not provide enough
water. Le Papet and Ugolin block the spring at Les Romarins,
which Le Papet hopes to buy cheap for the profitable carnation
production after the death of its owner.

Their plans are foiled by the arrival of the inheritor, the
hunchback Jean Cadoret, his wife and daughter, Manon. Jean's
endeavours to make the property pay are frustrated by lack of
water, and he eventually dies in an accident digging a well. As
Manon and her widowed mother leave Les Romarins, the little
girl happens to catch a glimpse of Le Papet and Ugolin
unblocking the spring. In tears of rage, she takes to the hills,
leaving Le Papet joyfully 'baptizing' Ugolin King of the
Carnations in the water gushing from the spring. End of Part I.

A coffin is being made. This first image of *Manon des Sources*
is a premonition of revenge. The village square's bubbling
fountain and basin full of water from a spring in the hills are no
longer safe. Nor is Le Papet, who now helps Ugolin with his
flourishing carnations at Les Romarins. Nor Ugolin, as he hides
away the money from a profitable deal with a middleman from
Antibes.

Manon is biding her time to avenge her father's death.

Manon had just turned fifteen, but she was bigger
than her age. With her mother's help, she did up old
theatrical costumes. Time had not spared the colour,
but the rich fabrics had kept their strength: so the
shepherdess ran through the *garrigue* in faded brocade dresses and boleros of washed out silk, and in
the rain wore the hood with gold fringes of the
Manon who sang.

Her mother once sang the role of Massenet's *Manon Lescaut*
and has now returned to the opera stage, leaving her daughter
to lead the wild life she loves. Manon tends a herd of goats,

makes bouquets of wild herbs to sell at Aubagne market, and traps birds to feed herself and Baptistine at their cave-dwelling.

She is shy and modest, like a mountain recluse. She hides up a tree from the new village schoolteacher, Bernard, an amateur geologist looking for minerals in the hills. Occasionally, she visits her father's grave to place wild flowers and play his mouth organ. And she bathes naked in a pool, dances like some pagan sprite with her goats, and voluptuously suns herself on a warm rock.

One day, attracted by the sound of the mouth organ, Ugolin discovers her secret bathing place. Hiding in the bushes, he watches her naked dance in an onanistic trance. Le Papet wheedles out Ugolin's secret, and cunningly sees that marriage to Manon will provide an heir to the considerable Soubeyran fortune.

Manon is disgusted by Ugolin's advances. Furthermore, she has proof that the spring at Les Romarins was blocked by Le Papet and Ugolin and that the village knew about it. Jean, however, was an outsider and the Law of Silence, like Sicilian Omerta (see no evil, hear no evil), prevailed. Discovering by accident the source of the village fountain's water supply, Manon blocks it and watches with relish the suffering caused by a terrible drought. At a village gathering she unmasks Le Papet and Ugolin for indirectly causing her father's death – and a witness admits having seen them block the spring. Ugolin commits suicide. Le Papet is disgraced.

Manon unblocks the spring as secretly as she blocked it and, like a miracle, water returns to the fountain.

After Manon's marriage to Bernard, Le Papet has a rendezvous with an old woman who was once the long-dead Florette's best friend. Why did Le Papet not reply to the letter from Florette saying she was pregnant by him? Because he was in Africa, military mail was unreliable, he never received it. Florette, says her friend, tried the Devil's magic to abort the baby. But it didn't work. The baby was born . . . with a hump. . .

Le Papet goes home and asks the Curé for the Last Rites. He gets dressed in his best suit, shaves and brushes his hair in the mirror. Surrounded by his souvenirs of Africa, he writes a letter to Manon, telling her he's her grandfather and asking her pardon. The treasure of the Soubeyrans will go to her son. The letter ends 'Adessias, pichounette'; Goodbye, little one. Le Papet dies peacefully in the night, absolved of his sins.

Claude Berri handles the final Dickensian twist and heightened emotions of Pagnol's epic without embarrassment. Disbelief is suspended by the confidence of his direction, the reality of the actors, and the authenticity of that secret Provence unknown to outsiders.

He was greatly helped by the insight of Pagnol's novels. It is the power of peasant money that defeats Jean de Florette's ecological ideals. Le Papet's deviousness and calculation are based on one simple philosophy: 'I am strong because I have a few *sous*.' Hypocrisy rules the lives of Bastidians. After complicity in Le Papet's killing of Pique-Bouffigue, Ugolin tells his nephew, Jean: 'He was a good friend, I used to run errands for him in the village. . .' The whole village turns up for the funeral of Jean de Florette, whom it did nothing to help: 'Then the Mayor greeted Aimée, and told her that he regretted not knowing her husband, and that the Commune would pay the expenses of the funeral. . .' And the outsider Baptistine makes a keen observation on hunting to feed yourself: 'As for those old maids who weep buckets about an innocent thrush or pretty finch, I haven't ever noticed them weeping over a lamb chop. . .'

Food and produce are minutely detailed. Le Papet wants Ugolin to harvest not just the humble chick pea, staple peasant diet, but two hundred trees each of fig, plum, apricot, and almond. He eats trout with Cassis wine, partridge with a Bordeaux, and brushes the dust off the local *jacquez* wine, twenty years old, saved for first communions and weddings. Less sophisticatedly, Manon shops free in her hills: *sanguins* and morel mushrooms, bitter *roquette* salad, and snails fed on wild thyme. For extolling Manon's beauty Pamphile, the village carpenter, gets his wife's mutton stew over his head – made with black olives, salt pork, and a sprig of *farigoule*, too.

Les Bastidians' faults are redeemed by humour and wit. Le Papet's three ways to ruin are: 'Women, gambling, and agriculture. Agriculture is the quickest and the least agreeable.'

Yves Montand, as Le Papet, gave a memorable last film performance. It was appropriate. Born in Marseilles of Italian parents, he had made his music hall debut at the Alcazar, where several of Pagnol's actors first appeared. He grew up with 'garlic and olive shows' and developed into a singer and actor of international renown, moving further and further from Marseilles. He starred in Hollywood with Marilyn Monroe and, most notably, as the truck-driver in Clouzot's *The Wages of Fear*.

Marcel Pagnol attended the wedding of Montand and Simone Signoret at St-Paul-de-Vence in 1942. As dedicated radicals, they were among the first Westerners to visit post-war Communist Russia, making frequent appearances there. Yves Montand also gave one-man shows at the Olympia Music Hall in Paris.

All this was a far cry from Provence. Returning to play Le Papet, Montand did not find it easy. The accent and mannerisms of the Midi did not return naturally. All the more credit to him that he eventually turned in one of the great performances of his career, subtle and totally convincing. He makes Le Papet age before our very eyes. From a spry old devil he becomes a broken old man. When he hears of Ugolin's suicide by hanging, Montand is at his most moving. Gently, he removes the love-charm ribbon Ugolin has sewn to his nipple, orders the finest oak for his coffin, and persuades the Mayor to keep the suicide a secret from the Curé so that his godson will have a Christian burial.

Daniel Auteil as Ugolin and Yves Montand as Le Papet in Jean de Florette.

Gérard Depardieu was at his loping, extravagant best as Jean de Florette and I must confess to missing his strong presence in *Manon des Sources*.

Ironic that Jean should turn out to be Le Papet's son, for as a former employee of the taxman, and a hunchback as well, he is all the old man fears and despises. 'Often a peasant becomes a

hunchback, it's rare that a hunchback becomes a peasant,' he comments. 'He puts on gloves to dig.' But Jean – in the beefy frame of Depardieu – has the guts and determination of a man with the soil in his blood. Although unsuitably clad for retiling a roof, in homburg hat and brocade waistcoat, Jean overcomes his deformity to pursue his dream. 'I want to live in communion with nature. I want to eat the vegetables of my garden, the oil of my olives, get drunk only on the wine of my vines, and as soon as possible, eat the bread I make with my wheat.'

Daniel Auteil as Ugolin and Gérard Depardieu as Jean de Florette.

Even when faced with penury, Jean never loses his faith in nature as provider: chick-peas, goat's milk and cheese, wild salad and game. 'That will be our diet for six months. Austere but healthy – and we know that success is at the end of it.'

Depardieu convinces us with his consuming passion. And later Pagnol evokes Jean's pleasure in achievement – the bookworm dandy with his manuals on roofing and plumbing, water-divining, crop rotation, rainfall statistics, and breeding Australian rabbits suddenly transformed into a practical, sweating, hard-labouring, hard-drinking man of the country. He had come home.

For the first time in his life, he had pleasure in living:
his mother had been born in this lonely farm, she
had, in her youth, beaten almonds from these almond
trees, stretched out her sheets in the grass beneath
these olive trees planted by ancestors two or three
centuries earlier. . . He loved these pine woods and
turpentine trees, the cuckoo in the morning, the spar-
row hawk at midday, the owls of evening, and while
he dug his land, beneath the swooping swallows, he
thought how not one of these creatures knew that he
was a hunchback (*Jean de Florette*).

The tragedy of Jean's fate at the hands of treacherous
neighbours and the vagaries of Midi weather is made all the
more poignant by the relish with which Depardieu portrays his
good life before the fall.

His performance could never have so truly evoked Provence's
duality without a beautifully judged, snake-in-the-grass protag-
onist in Daniel Auteuil as Ugolin, the friendly neighbour little
Manon sees through but her father blindly trusts. Auteuil was a
revelation – insidious, two-faced, pathetically manipulated by
Le Papet.

Ugolin fails to woo Manon, whom Le Papet sees as the
perfect wife for him: 'What we need is wide hips, long legs, and
nice big tits. Choose her like a mare to breed from.' And as she
happens also to be beautiful: 'That won't bother me; on the
contrary she will be La Belle Soubeyrane, and I shall enjoy
looking at her' (*Manon des Sources*).

For once in a Pagnol saga, life did not mirror art. Meeting on
this picture, Emmanuelle Béart (Manon) and Daniel Auteuil fell
in love and began living together. In her playing of Manon,
Emmanuelle Béart had not only natural beauty but a subtle
strength that turned what could have been a fey wimp into a
genuinely wild creature. And, in the smaller parts, Berri had
admirable support from fine Provençal actors like Armand
Meffre as the Mayor.

It is a great tribute to director Yves Robert that his 1988 *La
Gloire de Mon Père* and *Le Château de Ma Mère* were not
overshadowed by Berri's blockbusting duo. Robert had the
harder task; the material, described in Chapters II and III,
concerned a childhood seen through the rose-coloured glasses
of middle age. The lack of substantial dramatic conflict
threatened to make the memoirs too bland on screen. Masterful
at directing children (*The War of the Buttons*), Robert was
entirely successful with young Marcel (Julien Caimaca) and Lili

des Bellons (Joris Molinas). Philippe Caubère made a most *sympa* Joseph Pagnol, and you could see why Marcel adored his mother as played by the gorgeous Nathalie Roussel.

The final sequence of *La Château de Ma Mère* is a particularly effective twist, taken directly from Pagnol's book. There is a poignant last shot of the master walking at the Château de la Buzine, through the tangled undergrowth of the garden, shortly before his death. It had meant so much to him.

At the beginning of the Second World War, Pagnol had decided to make a Hollywood-en-Provence in the Marseilles area. He already had his location land near La Treille and the Prado studios in the city itself. He wished to expand. From his Paris base, he heard of an ideal château and grounds going begging. And, reckless in matters of property, without even asking its name he instructed his man-on-the-spot to buy it sight unseen.

On his first tour of inspection, imagine the shock of *déjà vu* when he realized where he was. It all came back to him: the scene of that furtive short-cut along the canal, and the confrontation with a brute of a caretaker who had frightened his mother into a faint.

> Yes, there it was. Sure enough, my childhood canal with its hawthorn, clematis, dog-rose full of white flowers, bramble-bushes hiding their thorns beneath big, grainy blackberries.
>
> All along the grassy path, water ran soundless, eternal, and grasshoppers from long ago sprang, like splashes of water, about my every step. Slowly I followed my holiday path again, and dear spirits were walking with me, close by. . .
>
> . . . through the branches of a dog-rose bush, beneath white buds and on the other side of time, there was a very young, dark-haired woman who, over the years, clasped the red roses the colonel had given her close to her fragile heart. She heard the shouts of the caretaker, and his dog's raucous panting. Pale, trembling, and forever inconsolable, she did not know she was at her son's house (*Le Château de Ma Mère*).

PAGNOL'S PROVENCE

The films of Claude Berri and Yves Robert were shot in some of the most enchanting locations you could wish to find in Provence.

Overleaf: La Gaude, near Aix-en-Provence – 'The Colonel's Château' in Yves Robert's film of Le Château de Ma Mère.

Berri opted for more greenery than is now evident in Pagnol's beloved **Chaîne de L'Étoile** hills. Devastation by six forest fires during the century (the work of lunatic pyromaniacs or unscrupulous property developers who can deal more easily in unforested land) has depleted the valleys of holm-oaks and Aleppo pines. Sensibly but sadly, the whole area is closed to visitors in the tinderbox months of July, August and half of September – the school holidays. What would Marcel have made of that?

Not far from Aubagne, just across the border of Bouches-du-Rhône and Var, is a Provençal Garden of Eden. Berri set up his headquarters at **Riboux**, the smallest commune in France (population: six).

He owed his good fortune to an Aubagne writer and old friend of Pagnol's, Georges Berni. And Berni kindly guided us in the steps of *Jean de Florette* and *Manon des Sources* – an enchanted trek of nine and a half miles on a perfect June day. We met only one other person; he was clearing undergrowth and looked very surprised to see us. If this does not seem a very amazing statistic in these days of short walks in the Hindu Kush, I should point out that our Garden of Eden is only ten miles due north of Bandol and the mass tourism of the Riviera coast. An even more amazing statistic was the age of our guide. Georges Berni was a sprightly eighty-one, setting the insistent, steady pace of a mountain goat.

On the Toulon road from Aubagne, just before **Cuges-les-Pins**, Berni pointed out a farmhouse in pine trees on the south-facing slope of the Massif de Ste-Baume. It had played Ugolin's **Mas de Massacan**. A hike up to the Pujeade *quartier*, as the area is known, takes an hour there and back from the main road.

Hearts sank as we turned left at the 'OK Corral' (a Western theme park) but rose again as we instantly entered *garrigue* of the purest, wildest beauty. You can get your bearings by **Mont Cuques**, which is shaped like a haystack – *cuques* in Provençal. On a track to our right before Riboux, we parked the car below Mont Cuques. Morning mists hung eerily over the thick pine woods to the south. In less than a square metre, Berni was able to point out all the principal *garrigue* vegetation: tufts of green and golden *baouco* grass, small green kermes-oaks alive with ladybirds, sumac and turpentine trees, juniper bushes, mauve and white cistus. The 'bean sickness' on a turpentine – little brown pods that explode – make it known in Provençal as 'the farting tree'. Scatological names are popular: the prickly dog-rose is known as 'scratch-arse' because dogs like to scratch their behinds on its prickles.

Walking up the course of a dried-up stream, we came to **Le Bassin de la Perdrix**, a reservoir fed by an underground stream, which Berri had specially constructed for the film. Running down the nearby slope, Manon hears the villagers talking as they clean out red bauxite which has come from the village's spring.

A pastoral landscape of woods, heathland, and poppy-filled fields leads to the Bastide de Châteaurenard. This fine, solid old farmhouse played **Le Mas des Romarins**. On one side Berri planted a small olive grove where Le Papet pulled Pique-Bouffigue from a tree for insulting the Soubeyrans, accidentally killing him; on the other side, Ugolin's carnations flourished; and in between were Jean de Florette's giant Australian rabbits which the villagers found so hilarious.

Interior scenes were shot at another *bastide* along the walk – La Peiresède – standing near a magnificent ancient oak with three trunks. The cistern sports a shaving mirror. In one memorable scene, Jean de Florette looks hopefully out of his bedroom window, hearing thunder. But the storm, as it so often does in the Midi, passes tantalizingly by and no rain relieves the dreadful drought. Jean's prayers have fallen on deaf ears. He yells at the clearing sky: 'Is there NO ONE there?'

We seemed to be walking through a yellow forest of genista. Above the **Gorges du Pousson**, a short climb to the top of a *barre* took us to **La Grotte du Mounoi**. Covered with ivy, the cave was hard to find even for Berni. Now an archaeological site, it is here that Manon, searching for a lost goat, accidentally finds the spring which feeds the village reservoir, recognizing it by the red bauxite.

The round-trip trek ended at our car, parked near **Le Charnier de Signes**. This memorial of melancholy beauty in the **Vallon des Martyrs** is a tribute to thirty-seven Resistance fighters, shot by the Nazis towards the end of hostilities. The massacre was witnessed by a shepherd who was too afraid to report it until after the war.

This trek should not be attempted without advice from the Aubagne Tourist Office (large-scale maps, a light picnic and water essential).

You can easily visit two of the châteaux filmed by Yves Robert. One is a bit of detour but well worth it: Le Château d'Astros at **Vidauban** (Var) played **Le Château de la Buzine** with suitable elegance. Join the excellent bus trip which goes from the Aix-en-Provence Tourist Office; it takes you to the Italianate country houses and gardens in the enchanting **Vallée des Pinchinats**.

One of them is Le Château de la Gaude, which played the **Notary's Château**.

Several locations are in the **South Lubéron**, which is infinitely more beautiful and less touristy than the 'Disneyland-en-Provence' on the other side of the hill. **Mirabeau**, on the Durance, was once the village of the famous revolutionary Comte Honoré de Mirabeau, whose love life in Aix was a Feydeau farce of dangerous liaisons. A great orator, he tried to get Louis XVI to accept a constitutional monarchy on English lines.

Here, Berri found a more imposing fountain and bigger village square than at La Treille. Also there was room to play *boules*, establish an outdoor café ambience, and parade the village saint round the dried-up fountain in hope of a miracle. Ironically, the fountain displays a notice: '*Défense de laver dans la fontaine sous peine d'amende*' (anyone washing in the fountain will be fined).

The Romanesque chapel near the south Lubéron village of Vaugines, where Manon's wedding photograph was taken in Manon des Sources.

The road from Mirabeau to **Grambois** takes you through a regional park, its agriculture confined to small fields, golden with maize and wheat, green with olives and vines. From around here comes the best Côtes du Lubéron wine, a fast-improving *appellation*.

Grambois became Yves Robert's La Treille, perched on a hill in the depths of the country, with no Marseilles sprawl to impede shooting. Joseph Pagnol played *boules* in the square and had his *bartavelles* weighed in the bakery, and Oncle Jules and Tante Rose went to church.

Star of this itinerary is **Ansouis**, dominated by a flag-flying château which has to be visited for its fabulous Provençal kitchen with a battery of gleaming copper pans. Nothing is excessively done up here, unlike Gordes and Le Castellet. It has charm, peace and quiet. The church was formerly part of the castle. In its elaborate, cool interior, Manon was married to the schoolmaster, Bernard, and the Curé gave a memorable Pagnolian sermon about the wrath of God falling on the Bastidians, cursed with a drought for their sins.

Manon's wedding photograph was taken outside the Romanesque chapel of **Vaugines**, situated romantically in a cherry orchard. Le Papet brought carnations to Ugolin's grave, and sat on a bench here to discover the awful truth about Jean de Florette's birth.

And last but not least, the little school of St-Loup – impossible now to find in the Marseilles suburb – was shot at **Charleval** near Mallemort on the river Durance. Its red-brick nineteenth-century façade with just one word '*École*', and its shady yard made it the perfect setting for Marcel's first precocious reading achievements, aged four and a half.

In the depths of this countryside, good hotels are rare. Probably the best are in the Albert Camus village of Lourmarin, which has a gem of a Renaissance château: Le Moulin de Lourmarin (expensive), and the country Hôtel de Guilles (moderate) on the Vaugines road with its restaurant, L'Agneau Gourmand.

B & Bs flourish at Grambois: Le Jas de Monsieur (moderate), an eighteenth-century *bastide* in Lubéron woods; and the Domaine de Piegros (moderate), a thirteenth-century monastic farm which also provides dinner.

My own choice would be Madame Rogers's Le Jardin d'Ansouis (moderate) at Ansouis. It is an old village house in the ramparts with a flowery courtyard for breakfast, and an inviting choice of *table d'hôte* menus (inexpensive/moderate).

SELECT BIBLIOGRAPHY

Adouard, Yvan, *Adouard reconte Pagnol* (Stock)

Berni, Georges, *Dans les pas de Marcel Pagnol*

—— *Marcel Pagnol – Enfant d'Aubagne et de la Treille*

—— *Merveilleux Pagnol* (Pastorelly)

Brun, Paulette, *Raimu, Mon Père* (Hachette)

Castans, Raymond, *Marcel Pagnol m'a raconté* (Editions de la Table Ronde)

—— *Marcel Pagnol* (Editions Jean-Claude Lattès)

Chabot, Jacques, *La Provence de Jean Giono* (Edisud)

Clébert, Jean-Paul, *La Provence de Pagnol* (Edisud)

D'Arnaud, *Evocation du Vieux Marseille* (Editions de Minuit)

Hatier, *Les Années Pagnol* (Forma-5 Continents)

Rim, Carlo, *Fernandel* (Kalman-Lévy)

Also the following works of Marcel Pagnol, mentioned in the text but not listed in the section 'Provence in Pagnol':

Le Boulanger Aimable – short story

Les Bucoliques de Virgile (Grasset) – French translation of Virgil

Cinématurgie de Paris (Editions de Fallois) – essays on the cinema

Jazz – play

Les Marchands de la Gloire – play (with Paul Nivoix)

La Prière des Étoiles – screenplay

Topaze – play

Videos of Pagnol films mentioned in the book are available in the Collection Marcel Pagnol produced by the Compagnie Mediterranéenne de Films, 9 r. de Vanvcs, 92100 Boulogne-Billancourt. Videos of Claude Berri's *Jean de Florette* and *Manon des Sources*, and Yves Robert's *La Gloire de Mon Père* and *Le Château de Ma Mère*, are also available.

INDEX
OF PLACES

Emmanuelle Béart as Manon in Claude Berri's film of Manon des Sources.